Legal & Disclaimer

The information contained in this book and its contents is not designed to replace or take the place of any form of medical or professional advice; and is not meant to replace the need for independent medical, financial, legal or other professional advice or services, as may be required. The content and information in this book has been provided for educational and entertainment purposes only.

The content and information contained in this book has been compiled from sources deemed reliable, and it is accurate to the best of the Author's knowledge, information and belief. However, the Author cannot guarantee its accuracy and validity and cannot be held liable for any errors and/or omissions. Further, changes are periodically made to this book as and when needed. Where appropriate and/or necessary, you must consult a professional (including but not limited to your doctor, attorney, financial advisor or such other professional advisor) before using any of the suggested remedies, techniques, or information in this book.

Introduction

There are so many diets that claim to have long-term benefits to people. It is therefore important that you constantly do due diligence on what diet works and what diet offers short-term results. One of the diet regimens that you might want to consider is the Optavia Diet. The Optavia Diet is one of the hottest trends of the many diet regimens that are available in the market. It is designed for people who want to achieve long-term weight loss. Moreover, this diet is also celebrated as one of the best diets in the United States. So, if you want to adopt this particular diet to enjoy its benefits, then this book will serve as your guide on what you need to know about the Optavia Diet.

CONTENTS

What Is the Optavia Diet?

The Optavia Diet provides convenience to people as it is a convenient meal replacement that removes the guesswork for many of its dieters. The Optavia Diet, previously known as Medifast, was developed by Dr. William Vitale and encourages people to eat healthy in order to achieve sustainable weight loss.

Under this diet regimen, dieters follow a weight plan including five fuelings a day as well as one lean green meal a day. One of the popular diet plans that Optavia has to offer is the 5&1 plan that is designed for rapid weight loss. With this diet plan, users need to eat five of Optavia's fuelings and one lean and green meal daily.

With the meal replacement and lean green meals, this diet is perfect for people who do not only want to lose weight but also for people who want to transition from their old unhealthy habits to a healthier one. Thus, this is perfect for people who suffer from gout, diabetes, as well as people who are in their senior years.

Because it is a commercial diet, it has been subjected to different studies involving its efficacy. Studies have noted that people can lose weight in as little as 8 weeks therefore this is one of the most efficient diet regimens there is that people can adapt and eventually embrace as part of their lifestyles. Read on to learn about the Optavia Diet.

What To Eat

Depending on the type of diet plan that you choose, you have to eat a number of lean and green meals that are comprised mainly of lean proteins and non-starchy vegetables. Although this diet regimen is not as restrictive as other diet regimens, this means that there are plenty of foods that are compliant to this diet including healthy fats. Thus, below are the types of foods that you can eat while following the Optavia Diet.

- **Optavia fuelings:** The Optavia Diet is famous for its Optavia fuelings that involve pre-packaged foods that dieters can eat. There are more than 60 soups, shakes, bars, and other fueling products that you can consume as your meal replacements.

- **Lean meats:** Lean and green meals require you to make foods out of lean meats. There are three categories of lean meats identified by Optavia including (1) lean, (2) leaner, and (3) leanest. Lean meats include salmon, pork chops, and lamb while leaner meats include chicken breasts and swordfish. Leanest meats include egg whites, shrimp, and cod.

- **Green and non-starchy vegetables:** Non-starchy vegetables are further identified into (1) lower carb, (2) moderate carb, and (3) higher carb. Lower carbs include all types of salad greens and green leafy vegetables. Moderate carb vegetables include summer squash and cauliflower. Lastly, high carb vegetables include peppers and broccoli.

- **Healthy fats:** Healthy fats are encouraged for people who follow the Optavia Diet. These include healthy fats such as olive oil, walnut oil, flaxseed, and avocado. However, it is important to consume two servings of healthy fats to still keep up with the Optavia Diet.

- **Others:** Once dieters are able to achieve their weight loss goals through meal replacements, they can start consuming other foods to maintain their ideal weight. These include low-fat dairy, fresh fruits, and whole grains. You can also consume meatless alternatives including 2 cups egg substitute, and 5 ounces seitan. For low-fat dairy, you are allowed to consume 1 ½ cups 1% cottage cheese and 12 ounces of non-fat Greek yogurt.

What Not to Eat

Similar to other diet regimens, the Optavia Diet also discourages dieters not to eat certain types of foods. This section will discuss the foods that are non-compliant to the principles of the Optavia Diet.

- **Indulgent desserts:** This diet regimen discourages the consumption of indulgent desserts such as cakes, ice cream, cookies, and all kinds of pastries. While eating these foods is discouraged during the first few weeks of following the diet, moderate consumption of sweet treats such as fresh fruits and yogurts can be integrated into one's diet.

- **Sugary beverages:** Similar to indulgent desserts, sugary beverages are also discouraged among those who follow the Optavia Diet. These include soda, fruit juices, and energy drinks.

- **Unhealthy fats:** Fats such as butter, shortening, and commercial salad dressings contain large amounts of calories that are not good for people who are trying to lose weight. Moreover, they also contain preservatives and salt that is not good for the overall health.

- **Alcohol:** Those who follow the Optavia Diet should limit their alcohol intake to 5 ounces of alcohol daily.

The Benefits of The Optavia Diet

The Optavia Diet has a high success rate especially among people who want to lose weight. But more than losing weight, there are so many benefits of following the Optavia Diet. Below are the many benefits that people can enjoy when following this particular diet.

- **Better for portion control:** Perhaps one of the most challenging facets of dieting is portion control. Many people find it difficult to control the amount of food while dieting but the Optavia Diet is really strict when it comes to its fueling phase as it strictly implements portion control thanks to its pre-packaged fueling foods.

- **Structured eating plan:** The Optavia Diet follows a structured eating plan thus making it very easy to follow. Everything is indicated on their website so you do not need to figure everything else on your own.

- **Builds a healthy relationship with food:** The problem with most people why they revert to their old eating habits is that they do not have a good relationship with food. But with the Optavia Diet, it is backed by a solid and supportive community that helps each other out. With the support of great people, it is easier for people to develop healthy eating habits as they gain appreciation for the many options and support that they have.

- **Better overall health:** The Optavia Diet was not only designed only for weight loss. In fact, it was also designed for people to achieve better overall health. Several studies have noted that this diet is also associated with lowering blood and sugar levels due to its limited Sodium intake.

How to Start the Optavia Diet?

The Optavia Diet has two unique phases: Initial and Maintenance Phases. Upon enrollment, you will be assigned a diet coach that will help you undertake all the necessary things in order to be a successful dieter. So, if you are wondering what are the steps that you need to undertake while following the two phases, then this section will discuss just that.

The initial phase is when people are encouraged to limit their calorie intake from 800 to 1,000 calories for the next 12 weeks or until the dieter loses 12 pounds. For this phase, dieters are encouraged to consume lean and green meals five to seven times daily. Moreover, dieters are also encouraged to consume 1 optional snack including sugar-free gelatin, celery sticks, and 12 ounces of nuts.

The maintenance phase, on the other hand, is implemented once you have already lost the 12 pounds from your initial weight. During this phase, you can increase your calorie intake to 1,550 daily. This phase can last for 6 weeks. Moreover, you are also allowed to incorporate other foods such as whole grains, fruits, and low-fat dairy into your diet.

After the maintenance phase, you are not ready to follow your specific Optavia Diet plan. This is also the time when you need to consume not only lean and green meals but also fueling foods. The number of meals depends on the specific diet plan you choose. For instance, if you opt for the 3&3 Optavia plan, you need to consume three lean and green meals and three fuelings.

How to Follow the Optavia Diet?

While the Optavia Diet is all about delivering weight loss to its dieters, the success of dieters still largely depends on how they approach this particular diet regimen. Thus, if you want to become successful, below are the tips that you should do while following the Optavia Diet.

- Opt for foods that are cooked using healthy cooking methods. Healthy cooking methods include baking, grilling, poaching, and broiling. Avoid frying your foods as cooking oil increases the calorie content of your food.

- Portion sizes of your food should follow the Optavia recommendations. This means that the portion sizes refer to the cooked weight and not the raw weight of the ingredients that you are using.

- Opt for foods that are rich in Omega-3 fatty acids such as tuna salmon, mackerel, trout, herring, and many other cold-water fishes. Omega-3 fatty acids contribute to lowering inflammation in the body.

- Choose meatless alternatives such as tofu and tempeh. They rich in proteins but not too much on calories.

- Following the program at all costs even if you are dining out. This means that you have to consume healthy meals when you eat out and make sure that you stay away from alcohol.

Following the Optavia Diet

The developers of the Optavia Diet strives to be transparent when it comes to developing their many regimens and plans. But if you have questions about this diet regimen, then below are some FAQs that many people ask.

Which Optavia Diet plan is good for me?
As there are so many diet plans offered by Optavia, it is important to get in touch with a certified Optavia coach to learn about the many options that you have. It is crucial that you do not second guess the diet plan that you are going to follow as each diet plan is designed to fit a particular profile. For instance, if you are a very active person, you can take on the Optavia 5&1 plan. But then, the coach will also look at other factors such as your age and health risks so that you can be matched with the right Optavia Diet Plan.

Can I skip the fuelings?
No. You must stick with fuelings if you want to successfully follow the Optavia Diet. Fuelings are designed to provide the body with balanced amounts of macronutrients that can promote an efficient fat-burning state to help people lose fat without losing energy. The problem if you skip fueling is that you may miss out on important nutrients that might lead to fatigue while following this diet. The body feels fatigued because it cannot compensate for the lack of nutrients while being calorie deficient.

Can I rearrange my fuelings?
Yes. If you are a busy person with a dynamic schedule, then you can rearrange the timing on when you will take your fueling meals. The Optavia Diet is not strict about rearranging meals as long as you consume your meals within 24 hours. This versatility on your eating schedule makes it perfect for people who also have unusual schedules including those who work at night or beyond regular working hours. So how do you time your fuelings? Just make sure that you eat your meals every two or three hours throughout the time that you are awake. Your first meal should be taken an hour after waking up to ensure optimal blood sugar levels. This is also great for hunger control.

Lean and Green Fish and Seafood Recipes

Pan-Seared Scallops and Zucchini Noodles

Serves: 2
Cooking Time: 10 minutes

Ingredients:
6 ounces jarred roasted red peppers, drained and chopped
½ cup unsweetened cashew milk
2 ounces avocado
2 teaspoons lemon juice
1 clove garlic, minced
¼ teaspoon salt
2 small zucchinis, ends removed and spiralized
¼ teaspoon olive oil
1-pound raw scallops

Directions:
1) Place the roasted red peppers, cashew milk, avocado, lemon juice, garlic, and salt in a blender. Pulse until smooth. Set aside.
2) Place the zucchini in a plate and pour over the prepared sauce.
3) Brush a pan with olive oil and over medium flame. Season the scallops with salt.
4) Sear all sides of the scallops for 3 to 5 minutes on each side.
5) Serve the scallops on top of the zucchini noodles.

Nutrition Information:
Calories per serving: 265; Protein:31.1 g; Carbs: 19.9g; Fat: 7.3g Sugar: 7.2g

Salmon Burgers with Cucumber Salad

Serves: 2
Cooking Time: 25 minutes

Ingredients:
1 egg, beaten
1 ½ tablespoon light mayonnaise
½ teaspoon lemon juice
¼ teaspoon dried parsley
1.5 ounce can drained pink salmon, shredded
1 packet multigrain crackers, crushed
1 5 ounces low-fat plain Greek yogurt
2 tablespoons apple cider vinegar
1 tablespoon fresh dill, chopped
A dash of salt and pepper
3 cups thinly sliced cucumber

Directions:

1) Place the egg, mayonnaise, lemon juice, parsley, salmon, and crackers in a bowl. Mix until well combined. Form two patties using your hands. Place on a baking sheet lined with parchment paper.
2) Place in a 350°F preheated oven and cook for 25 minutes until lightly golden.
3) While cooking the burgers, mix the remaining ingredients in a bowl and toss to coat.
4) Serve the burgers with cucumber salad.

Nutrition Information:
Calories per serving: 210; Protein: 14.4g; Carbs: 11.4g; Fat: 11.9g Sugar: 7.1g

Salmon Florentine

Serves: 4
Cooking Time: 30 minutes

Ingredients:
½ cup chopped green onion
1 teaspoon olive oil
2 garlic cloves, minced
1 12 ounces packaged frozen chopped spinach
1 ½ cups chopped celery
¼ teaspoon crushed red pepper flakes
Salt and pepper to taste
½ cup part-skim ricotta cheese
4 5 ½ ounces wild salmon filets

Directions:
1) Preheat the oven to 350°F.
2) Heat skillet over medium flame and cook the green onions and olive oil. Add the garlic and cook for another 30 seconds. Stir in the spinach, celery, red pepper flakes, and season with salt and pepper to taste. Stir for 3 minutes until the spinach has wilted. Turn off the heat and set aside to cool slightly.
3) Mix the ricotta cheese into the cooked spinach. Mix until well-combined.
4) Place the salmon on a parchment-lined baking sheet. Top the salmon with the ricotta and spinach mixture.
5) Place in the oven for 30 minutes.

Nutrition Information:
Calories per serving: 145; Protein: 15g; Carbs: 8.6g; Fat: 6.3g Sugar: 2.2g

Shrimp and Cauliflower Grits

Serves: 2
Cooking Time: 20 minutes

Ingredients:
1-pound raw shrimps, peeled and deveined
½ tablespoon Cajun seasoning
Cooking spray
1 tablespoon lemon juice
¼ cup chicken broth
1 tablespoon butter
2 ½ cups cauliflower, grated or minced finely
½ cup unsweetened cashew milk
¼ teaspoon salt
2 tablespoons sour cream
1/3 cup reduced fat shredded cheddar cheese
¼ cup sliced scallions

Directions:
1) Place the shrimps and Cajun seasonings into a Ziploc bag and close the bag. Toss to coat the shrimps evenly with the seasoning.
2) Spray a skillet with cooking spray and cook the seasoned shrimps until pink. This will take about 2 to 3 minutes per side. Add the lemon juice and chicken broth. Make sure to scrape the bottom to remove the browned bits. Set aside.
3) In another skillet, heat butter over medium flame and add the riced cauliflower. Cook for 5 minutes and add the milk and salt. Cook for another 5 minutes. Remove from the heat and add the sour cream, and cheese. Stir until well-combined.
4) Serve the shrimps on top of the cauliflower grits.
5) Garnish with scallions.

Nutrition Information:
Calories per serving: 456; Protein: 63.5g; Carbs: 13.8g; Fat: 15.3g Sugar: 6.5g

Tuna Niçoise Salad

Serves: 4
Cooking Time: 10 minutes

Ingredients:
4 teaspoons extra virgin olive oil
3 tablespoons balsamic vinegar
2 garlic gloves, minced
6 cups mixed greens
2 cups string beans, steamed
1 cup cherry tomatoes, halved
6 hard-boiled eggs, sliced
2 7 ounces can of tuna, packed in water and drained

Directions:
1) Mix the oil, vinegar, and garlic in a bowl until well combined.
2) Place the remaining ingredients in a bowl and drizzle with the prepared sauce.

Nutrition Information:
Calories per serving: 392; Protein: 36.6g; Carbs:18.6 g; Fat: 19.2g Sugar: 9.5g

Savory Salmon with Cilantro

Serves: 4
Cooking Time: 30 minutes

Ingredients:
4 cups fresh cilantro, divided
2 tablespoons fresh lemon or lime juice
2 tablespoons red pepper sauce
1 teaspoon cumin
½ teaspoon salt
½ cup water
4 7 ounces raw salmon filets
6 cups bell pepper (all colors), seeded and julienned
½ teaspoon pepper
Cooking spray

Directions:
1) Place half the cilantro, lemon juice, red pepper sauce, cumin, salt, and water in a blender. Pulse until smooth. Transfer into a Ziploc bag and place the salmon. Marinate for 1 hour inside the fridge.
2) Preheat the oven to 400°F. Arrange the bell peppers in a lightly-greased baking dish. Sprinkle with pepper and bake for 10 minutes.
3) Drain the salmon and place on top of the pepper slices and bake for 20 minutes.
4) Garnish with the remaining cilantro.

Nutrition Information:
Calories per serving: 341; Protein: 42.9g; Carbs: 8.4g; Fat: 14.6g Sugar: 4g

Middle Eastern Salmon with Tomatoes and Cucumber

Serves: 4
Cooking Time: 30 minutes

Ingredients:
4 cups sliced cucumber
1-pint cherry tomatoes, halved
¼ cup cider vinegar
½ cup fresh dill, chopped
Salt and pepper to taste
1 ½ pounds skinless salmon
1 tablespoon Za'atar sauce
4 lemon wedges for garnish

Directions:
1) Preheat the oven to 350°F.
2) Place the cucumber and tomatoes in a bowl. Add in the vinegar, dill, and season with salt and pepper to taste. Toss to coat.
3) Season the salmon with Za'atar on both sides and place in a foil-lined baking sheet. Roast until the internal temperature reaches to 145°F.
4) Serve the roasted salmon with the cucumber and tomatoes.

Nutrition Information:
Calories per serving: 282; Protein: 35.7g; Carbs: 5.4 g; Fat: 12.4g Sugar: 2.4g

Low-Carb Lobster Roll

Serves: 4
Cooking Time: 10 minutes

Ingredients:
2 small hearts romaine lettuce
1 tablespoon butter, melted
1/3 cup plain low-fat Greek yogurt
2 tablespoons olive oil-based mayonnaise
1 small celery stalk, chopped
2 teaspoons lemon juice
1 tablespoon chopped chives
¼ teaspoon Old Bay seasoning
Salt and pepper to taste
12 ounces cooked lobster meat

Directions:
1) Preheat the grill to 350°F.
2) Slice the romaine hearts lengthwise and remove the inner leaves from each halved lettuce to create a boat-like shape where the lobster fillings will be put. Brush the insides of the lettuce with butter and grill cut-side down for 3 minutes. Set aside.
3) In a medium bowl, combine the rest of the ingredients. Mix until well-combined.
4) Place the lobster in the middle of the cooked lettuce halved. Serve immediately.

Nutrition Information:
Calories per serving: 338; Protein: 33.8g; Carbs: 34.4g; Fat: 8.8g Sugar: 2.1g

Steamed White Fish Tacos

Serves: 2
Cooking Time:15 minutes

Ingredients:
1-pound raw cod filets
½ teaspoon garlic powder
½ teaspoon salt, divided
½ cup diced tomato
2 tablespoons chopped red onion
½ jalapeno pepper, chopped
2 tablespoons chopped fresh cilantro
1 tablespoon lime juice
6 ounces avocado, sliced and meat scooped out
6 large romaine lettuce leaves

Directions:
1) Season the cod with garlic powder and salt. Steam the fish for 10 minutes. Flake the fish using a fork and remove any bones. Set aside to cool.
2) In a bowl, combine the tomatoes, onions, jalapeno pepper, cilantro, and lime juice.
3) Assemble the tacos.
4) Layer the fish, tomato mixture, and avocado on top of the lettuce leaves.
5) Serve immediately.

Nutrition Information:
Calories per serving: 426; Protein: 37.4g; Carbs: 78.4g; Fat: 16.7g Sugar: 3g

Blackened Shrimps with Salad Lettuce

Serves: 4
Cooking Time: 6 minutes

Ingredients:
2 pounds raw shrimps, peeled and deveined
1 tablespoon Old Bay Blackened Seasoning
4 teaspoons olive oil, divided
1 cup plain 2% Greek yogurt
6 ounces avocado
2 tablespoons lime juice, divided
1 ½ cups diced tomatoes
¼ cup diced green bell pepper
¼ cup chopped red onion
1 chopped jalapeno pepper
12 large romaine lettuce, torn

Directions:
1) Season the shrimps with the Old Bay seasoning and place in a plastic bag to marinate in the fridge for 1 hour.
2) Heat two teaspoons of olive oil in a skillet and add the shrimps. Cook for 3 minutes until the shrimps are slightly pink. Set aside.
3) Combine the yogurt and avocado. Season with lime juice and pulse in a blender until smooth.
4) In a bowl, combine the rest of the ingredients and add the shrimp. Spread over the sauce.
5) Toss to coat.

Nutrition Information:
Calories per serving: 390; Protein: 50g; Carbs: 10.8g; Fat: 16g Sugar: 5.3g

Shrimp Scampi

Serves: 4
Cooking Time: 25 minutes

Ingredients:
1 small spaghetti squash, cut in half and seeds removed
2 ½ tablespoons olive oil
1 clove of garlic, minced
1 ¾ pound peeled and deveined shrimps
1 cup cherry tomatoes, halved
½ teaspoon crushed red pepper flakes
1 teaspoon lemon juice
1 tablespoon dried parsley
½ teaspoon onion powder
Salt and pepper to taste
¼ cup shredded Parmesan cheese

Directions:
1) Place the spaghetti squash in a steamer and steam for 20 minutes until tender. Allow to cool and scoop the flesh using fork. Set aside.
2) Heat oil in a skillet over medium flame and sauté the garlic for 30 seconds or until fragrant. Stir in the shrimps and stir for 1 minute. Add in the tomatoes, pepper flakes, lemon juice, dried parsley, onion powder, and salt and pepper to taste. Stir for 3 minutes.
3) Pour the shrimps on top of the cooked spaghetti squash.
4) Garnish with parmesan cheese.

Nutrition Information:
Calories per serving: 336; Protein: 43.6g; Carbs:9.5g; Fat: 13.1g Sugar: 6.2g

Shrimp Cobb Salad

Serves: 1
Cooking Time: 10 minutes

Ingredients:
2 cups romaine lettuce, cleaned and torn
4 ounces cooked and peeled shrimps
½ cup cherry tomatoes, halved
1 hard-boiled egg, sliced
1/8 avocado, diced
1 tablespoon ranch dressing

Directions:
1) Place all ingredients in a bowl and toss to combine everything.
2) Serve immediately.

Nutrition Information:
Calories per serving: 366; Protein: 34g; Carbs:7.9 g; Fat: 22g Sugar: 3.2g

Lemon-Garlic Scallops

Serves: 1
Cooking Time: 15 minutes

Ingredients:
7 ounces scallops
1 teaspoon olive oil
½ teaspoon garlic powder
1 tablespoon lemon juice

Directions:
1) Preheat the oven to 400°F.
2) Place all ingredients in a Ziploc bag and allow to marinate in the fridge for 1 hour.
3) Place the scallops on a foil-lined baking sheet.
4) Bake in the oven for 15 minutes.

Nutrition Information:
Calories per serving: 185; Protein: 24.26g; Carbs: 8.5g; Fat: 5.5g Sugar: 0.4g

Mustard Glazed Salmon

Serves: 4
Cooking Time: 20 minutes

Ingredients:
1 ¾ pounds salmon filets, cut int 6 equal pieces
¼ cup fish or chicken broth
2 tablespoons Dijon mustard
1 tablespoon low-sodium soy sauce
½ teaspoon pepper to taste

Directions:
1) Preheat the oven to 425°F.
2) Arrange the salmon slices in a baking dish.
3) In a bowl, mix together the broth, Dijon mustard, soy sauce, and pepper.
4) Brush the salmon with the sauce.
5) Bake for 20 minutes until the salmon becomes flaky.

Nutrition Information:
Calories per serving: 655; Protein: 121g; Carbs: 1.3g; Fat: 23g Sugar: 0.4g

Fire Cracker Shrimp

Serves: 1
Cooking Time: 3 minutes

Ingredients:
2 tablespoons apricot preserves, unsweetened
1 teaspoon lite soy sauce
¼ teaspoon crushed red pepper flakes
½ ounce raw, peeled shrimp
1 teaspoon olive oil

Directions:
1) Place the apricot preserves in a bowl and mash. Add the soy sauce and red pepper flakes. Thread the shrimps on a wooden skewer and brush with oil and the apricot preserves.
2) Grill for 3 minutes on each side.

Nutrition Information:
Calories per serving: 128; Protein: 1.1g; Carbs: 20.1g; Fat: 5.6g Sugar: 17.7g

Seared Scallops with Cauliflower Puree

Serves: 1
Cooking Time: 16 minutes

Ingredients:
9 ounces dry scallops
1/8 teaspoon lemon pepper
1/8 teaspoon coriander
1 teaspoon olive oil
½ teaspoon fresh chopped chives
1 ½ cups cauliflower florets
2 light cheese, of any choice
A dash of salt and pepper to taste

Directions:
1) Pat dry the scallops and season with lemon pepper, coriander, olive oil, and chives.
2) Spray cooking oil on a skillet and sear the scallops for 3 minutes on each side. Set aside.
3) Bring a pot of salted water to a boil and add in the cauliflower florets for 10 minutes.
4) Place the cooked cauliflower in a blender and add in the cheese. Season with salt and pepper to taste. Pulse until smooth.
5) Serve the scallops with the cauliflower puree.

Nutrition Information:
Calories per serving: 441; Protein: 44.2g; Carbs: 25.9g; Fat: 18.3g Sugar: 9.8g

Mexican Shrimp Bowl

Serves: 1
Cooking Time: 10 minutes

Ingredients:
½ pound shrimps, peeled and deveined
1/8 teaspoon cumin
1/8 teaspoon paprika
1/8 teaspoon dried oregano
Salt and pepper to taste
1 red onion, chopped
1 small lettuce head, torn
¼ cup green beans, blanched
¼ cup cherry tomatoes, halved
2 tablespoons lemon juice
1 hard-boiled egg, sliced

Directions:

1) Season the shrimps with cumin, paprika, oregano, salt, and pepper. Allow to marinate in the fridge for at least 1 hour.
2) Spray cooking oil on a skillet and cook the shrimps for 2 to 3 minutes on each side. Set aside.
3) Place the onion, lettuce, green beans, and tomatoes in a bowl. Add in the shrimps. Season with salt and lemon juice. Toss to coat.
4) Garnish with egg slices on top.

Nutrition Information:
Calories per serving: 458; Protein: 60.3g; Carbs: 23.6g; Fat: 13.6g Sugar: 10.5g

Teriyaki Halibut with Zucchini

Serves: 1
Cooking Time: 15 minutes

Ingredients:
7 ounces halibut filet
1/8 teaspoon salt
¼ teaspoon pepper
2 teaspoons teriyaki sauce
1 teaspoon olive oil
1 cup zucchini squash, sliced
½ teaspoon cayenne pepper

Directions:
1) Sprinkle the halibut filet with salt, pepper, and teriyaki sauce.
2) Place on a foil-lined baking sheet and bake in a 350°F preheated oven for 10 minutes. Remove from the oven and allow the fish to rest.
3) Heat oil in a skillet over medium flame and add in the squash. Season with salt and cayenne pepper.
4) Continue stirring for at least 3 minutes until the zucchini is cooked.
5) Serve the halibut with the sauteed zucchini.

Nutrition Information:
Calories per serving: 429; Protein: 29.7g; Carbs: 13.7g; Fat: 10.2g Sugar: 2.6g

Ancho Tilapia and Cauliflower Rice

Serves: 4
Cooking Time: 20 minutes

Ingredients:
4 tilapia filets
½ teaspoon salt
½ teaspoon ground ancho chili pepper
½ teaspoon cayenne pepper
½ teaspoon dried oregano
¼ teaspoon garlic powder
¼ teaspoon ground cumin
1 teaspoon lime juice
1 large head cauliflower, cut into florets

Directions:
1) Preheat the oven to 350°F.
2) Season the tilapia filets with salt, ancho chili pepper, cayenne pepper, oregano, garlic powder, and cumin.
3) Place the seasoned tilapia on a baking sheet lined with foil.
4) Bake for 20 minutes or until the tilapia becomes flaky.
5) Heat a pot of water and add a teaspoon of salt. Boil for 6 minutes then drain the cauliflowers. Place in ice water bath to arrest the cooking process.
6) Place the drained cauliflower in a food processor and pulse until the consistency turns gritty. Season with salt and pepper to taste.
7) Serve the tilapia with the cauliflower rice.

Nutrition Information:
Calories per serving: 131; Protein: 24.7g; Carbs: 6.7g; Fat: 2.2g Sugar: 1.3g

Dijon Salmon Cakes with Arugula and Capers

Serves: 2
Cooking Time: 20 minutes

Ingredients:
10 ounces canned boneless pink salmon, drained
2 eggs, beaten
2 teaspoons minced scallions
¾ teaspoons lemon zest
3 ½ teaspoon Greek yogurt
1 teaspoon Dijon mustard
½ teaspoon white horse radish
1 teaspoon capers, chopped
1 teaspoon lemon juice
2 cups baby arugula

Directions:
1) In a bowl, combine the canned salmon, eggs, scallions, lemon zest, Greek yogurt, Dijon mustard, and white horse radish. Stir to combine everything and form two cakes using your hands.
2) Place on a foil-lined baking sheet and allow to set in the fridge for at least 3 hours.
3) Bake in a 350°F preheated oven for at least 20 minutes.
4) Meanwhile, mix together the capers, lemon juice, and arugula. Season with salt and pepper to taste.
5) Serve the salmon cakes with the arugula and capers.

Nutrition Information:
Calories per serving: 346; Protein: 44.1g; Carbs: 3.9g; Fat: 17.1g Sugar: 2.1g

Lean and Green Meatless Recipes

Spaghetti Squash Gratin

Serves: 2
Cooking Time: 60 minutes

Ingredients:
1 2 ½ pounds spaghetti squash
2 eggs
1 cup reduced fat cheddar cheese, shredded
½ cup plain low-fat Greek yogurt
2 cloves garlic, minced
Salt and pepper to taste
½ cup reduced fat grated parmesan cheese

Directions:

1) Preheat the oven to 400°F.
2) Halve the spaghetti squash and scoop out the seeds. Put squash face down on a baking sheet lined with foil. Place in the oven and cook for 30 minutes. Allow to cool before scooping the meat and placing in a large bowl.
3) In another bowl, combine the remaining ingredients. Mix well until well combined.
4) Spread in a casserole dish and bake for 30 more minutes in the oven.

Nutrition Information:
Calories per serving: 503; Protein: 36.8g; Carbs: 41.4g; Fat: 22.8g Sugar: 19g

Veggie Dips and Buffalo Dip

Serves: 4
Cooking Time: 20 minutes

Ingredients:
1 tablespoon olive oil
2 teaspoons lemon juice
½ teaspoon salt
½ teaspoon pepper
½ teaspoon rosemary
4 cups sliced yellow squash
3 cups sliced zucchini
4 light spreadable cheese wedges
1 ½ cup plain low-fat Greek yogurt
¼ cup light ranch dressing
¼ cup light ranch dressing

Directions:
1) Preheat the oven to 400°F.
2) In a bowl, put the oil, lemon juice, salt, pepper, rosemary, and vegetables. Toss to coat the vegetables.
3) Arrange the vegetables in a baking sheet in a single layer.
4) Bake for 20 minutes until crisp.
5) Meanwhile, place the remaining ingredients in a bowl. Whisk to combine the dip.
6) Serve the crispy vegetables with the dip.

Nutrition Information:
Calories per serving: 140; Protein: 5g; Carbs: 15g; Fat: 4g Sugar: 2g

Grilled Tempeh with Eggplants and Watercress

Serves: 4
Cooking Time: 30 minutes

Ingredients:
20 ounces tempeh, sliced into large chunks
4 ½ cups diced eggplants
½ tablespoons rice vinegar
½ teaspoon ground black pepper
½ teaspoon salt, divided
1 ½ cups watercress
¼ cup minced scallions
½ cup fresh tomatoes, sliced
½ tablespoon lemon juice
1 ½ tablespoon soy sauce
1 teaspoon lime juice

Directions:
1) Pour boiling water over the tempeh and allow to soak for 30 minutes.
2) In a bowl, toss the eggplant together with the rice vinegar, pepper, and a quarter of the salt.
3) Fire the grill to 425°F and roast the seasoned eggplants for 30 minutes on all sides until golden brown and tender.
4) Remove the roasted eggplants and allow to cool.
5) Pat dry the tempeh and grill for 2 minutes on each side until golden brown. Set aside to cool.
6) Prepare the watercress salad by combining the remaining ingredients in a bowl. Toss to coat.
7) Serve the tempeh, grilled eggplants, and watercress together.

Nutrition Information:
Calories per serving: 310; Protein: 28g; Carbs: 20g; Fat:10 g Sugar: 2g

Zucchini and Tomato Skillet

Serves: 3
Cooking Time: 10 minutes

Ingredients:

1 teaspoon olive oil
1 clove garlic, minced
1 ½ cups tomatoes, peeled and diced
½ teaspoon salt
½ teaspoon dried basil
A dash of pepper
3 cups zucchini slices
1 ½ teaspoon grated fat-reduced parmesan cheese

Directions:

1) Heat oil in a skillet over medium flame and sauté the garlic for 30 seconds or until fragrant. Add in the tomatoes and stir for 1 minute.
2) Add in salt, basil, pepper, and zucchini slices.
3) Lower the heat to medium low and stir for another 5 minutes.
4) Turn off the heat and garnish with parmesan cheese before serving.

Nutrition Information:

Calories per serving: 91; Protein: 5.6g; Carbs: 5.4g; Fat: 5.5g Sugar: 3.1g

Grilled Tofu and Zucchini

Serves: 6
Cooking Time: 10 minutes

Ingredients:
3 ½ pounds firm tofu, sliced
2 teaspoons extra virgin olive oil, divided
1 teaspoon crushed garlic
2 teaspoons balsamic vinegar
1 zucchini, sliced to ¼ inch thick
Salt and pepper to taste

Directions:
1) Preheat the grill to 425°F.
2) Place all ingredients in a bowl and toss to coat both tofu slices and zucchini with the seasoning.
3) Place the zucchini and tofu on the grill and cook for 5 minutes on each side.
4) Serve immediately.

Nutrition Information:
Calories per serving: 395; Protein: 41.9g; Carbs: 12.5g; Fat: 23.7g Sugar: 0.7g

Zucchini Pasta Salad

Serves: 3
Cooking Time: 6 minutes

Ingredients:
Cooking spray
½ pound tofu, sliced
6 small zucchinis, spiralized
¼ cup sliced red onion
¼ cup cherry tomatoes, halved
1 green bell pepper, seeded and chopped
¼ cup green olives, pitted and sliced
12 ounce can heart of palm, drained
Fresh parsley, chopped
¼ cup apple cider vinegar
¼ cup extra virgin olive oil
½ tablespoon garlic powder
½ tablespoon Italian powder
½ teaspoon Dijon mustard
Salt and pepper to taste

Directions:
1) Spray cooking oil in a skillet over medium flame. Fry the tofu slices until golden brown and crispy. Set aside.
2) In a salad bowl, place the zucchini, red onion, cherry tomatoes, bell pepper, olives, hearts of palm, and parsley. Top with the crispy tofu.
3) In another bowl, combine the remaining ingredients. Whisk to create the sauce.
4) Drizzle over the vegetables.

Nutrition Information:
Calories per serving: 450; Protein: 18.4g; Carbs: 46.5g; Fat: 23.6g Sugar: 27.8g

Zucchini Ravioli

Serves: 4
Cooking Time: 20 minutes

Ingredients:
4 medium zucchinis
2 cups part-skim ricotta
1 2/3 cups shredded reduced-fat Italian blend cheese, divided
¼ cup reduced-fat parmesan cheese
1 egg
2 teaspoons lemon zest
1 clove garlic, minced
¼ teaspoon nutmeg
¼ teaspoon salt
1 ½ cups Italian tomato sauce
Cooking spray

Directions:
1) Preheat the oven to 375°F.
2) Slice the zucchini lengthwise to create two flat sides. Use a mandolin or peeler to slice the zucchini into thin strips.
3) In a bowl, combine the ricotta cheese, half of the Italian blend cheese, parmesan cheese, egg, lemon zest, garlic, and nutmeg.
4) Lay two strips of zucchini noodles such that they overlap lengthwise. Lay two more zucchini strips perpendicular to the two strips you have made to create a T shape. Spoon one tablespoon of heaping tablespoon. Bring the ends of the bottom two strips and fold over the ricotta mixture. Do the same thing on the other ends. Secure with toothpick and place in a baking dish.
5) Pour on top the tomato sauce and sprinkle with parmesan cheese on top.
6) Place in the oven and cook for 20 minutes.

Nutrition Information:
Calories per serving: 379; Protein: 30.6g; Carbs: 14.1g; Fat: 22.9g Sugar: 4.2g

Spaghetti Squash Waffle Grilled Cheese

Serves: 2
Cooking Time: 15minutes

Ingredients:
3 cups cooked spaghetti squash, meat only
2 eggs
1/3 cup grated parmesan cheese, low fat and low sodium
1/8 teaspoon salt
1 cup reduced fat shredded pepper jack cheese

Directions:
1) Place cooked squash meat in a clean cheesecloth and squeeze as much liquid as possible. Place in a bowl.
2) Add in the rest of the ingredients. Mix well to combine.
3) Preheat a waffle iron to medium high and spread the mixture in an even layer. Close the waffle iron and allow to cook for 10 minutes or until golden.
4) Serve hot.

Nutrition Information:
Calories per serving: 419; Protein: 29.1g; Carbs: 20.2g; Fat: 25.7g Sugar: 6.9g

Portobello Mushroom Pizzas

Serves: 1
Cooking Time: 10 minutes

Ingredients:
2 2 ounces Portobello mushroom, stems removed and gills scraped out
¼ cup Italian tomato sauce
4 ounces reduced fat shredded mozzarella cheese
2 tablespoons shredded basil

Directions:
1) Preheat the broiler to medium high heat.
2) Place the mushroom caps on a greased baking sheet lined with foil.
3) Broil fir 4 minutes until tender.
4) Spread the tomato sauce into each and top with cheese and basil.
5) Broil for another 3 minutes.

Nutrition Information:
Calories per serving: 511; Protein:47.7 g; Carbs: 92.8g; Fat: 1.3g Sugar: 6.4g

Zucchini Spinach Manicotti

Serves: 4
Cooking Time: 45 minutes

Ingredients:
2 large zucchinis
1 ½ cups part-skimmed ricotta cheese
1 egg, beaten
1 cup frozen spinach, thawed
1 ½ cups reduced fat shredded mozzarella cheese, divided
¼ cup grated parmesan cheese
1/8 teaspoon salt
A pinch of nutmeg
1 cup low sugar tomato sauce

Directions:

1) Preheat the oven to 375°F.
2) Use a mandolin to slice the zucchini into flat strips. Set aside.
3) In a bowl, combine the ricotta cheese, egg, spinach, ½ cup mozzarella cheese, parmesan, salt and nutmeg.
4) Layer the zucchini slices parallel to each other in a baking dish and place spoonful of ricotta cheese on top. Roll the zucchini and place the stuffed zucchini in a greased baking dish.
5) Pour the tomato sauce on top.
6) Sprinkle with the remaining cheese and bake for 25 minutes.

Nutrition Information:
Calories per serving:333; Protein: 27.4g; Carbs: 12.5g; Fat: 20.1g Sugar: 3.1g

Lean and Green Veggie Soup

Serves: 8
Cooking Time: 30 minutes

Ingredients:
½ head cabbage, chopped
3 cups chopped broccoli
1 cup diced carrots
8 stalks, celery
1 cup diced onion
1 cup chopped radishes
½ cup diced red bell pepper
½ cup diced red bell pepper
2 tablespoons minced garlic
6 ounces tomato paste
14-ounce can dice tomatoes
6 ½ cups water
1 teaspoon dried parsley
1 teaspoon turmeric
½ cup kale
Salt and pepper to taste

Directions:
1) Place ingredients except for the kale, salt and pepper in a soup pan.
2) Bring mixture to a boil and lower the heat to simmer for 30 minutes.
3) Remove from the heat and stir in the kale. Season with salt and pepper to taste.

Nutrition Information:
Calories per serving: 114; Protein: 6g; Carbs: 26g; Fat: 1g Sugar: 3g

Creamy Mashed Cauliflower and Gravy

Serves: 4
Cooking Time: 10 minutes

Ingredients:
4 cups cauliflower florets
¼ cup light cream cheese, softened
1 tablespoon unsalted butter
1 clove garlic, minced
1 teaspoon fresh rosemary
Salt and pepper to taste
3 tablespoons 30% less sodium brown gravy
¾ cup cold water

Directions:
1) Bring a pot of water into boil and add the cauliflower florets. Boil for 3 minutes then drain.
2) Place cooked cauliflowers in a food processor and pulse until smooth.
3) Prepare the gravy according to package directions.
4) Serve the mashed cauliflower with the gravy.

Nutrition Information:
Calories per serving: 94; Protein:3.5 g; Carbs: 7.2g; Fat: 6.6g Sugar: 3.2g

Kale and Red Pepper Egg Muffins

Serves: 4
Cooking Time: 30 minutes

Ingredients:
9 eggs, beaten
1 cup liquid egg whites
¾ cup plain low-fat Greek yogurt
Salt and pepper to taste
1 cup chopped kale
1 cup red bell pepper, chopped

Directions:
1) Preheat the oven to 375°F.
2) Whisk the eggs and egg whites until fluffy. Add in the rest of the ingredients.
3) Pour egg mixture in greased muffin tins.
4) Place in the oven and bake for 25 minutes.

Nutrition Information:
Calories per serving: 363; Protein: 29.2g; Carbs: 9.5g; Fat: 22.5g Sugar: 7.4g

Green Beans Casserole

Serves: 4
Cooking Time: 30 minutes

Ingredients:
1 16 ounces frozen whole green beans
Cooking spray
2 cups mushrooms, chopped
¼ cup diced yellow onions
1 clove garlic, minced
¾ cup non-fat plain Greek yogurt
¼ cup reduced fat sour cream
Salt and pepper to taste
½ cup reduced fat cheddar cheese, shredded

Directions:
1) Preheat the oven to 350°F.
2) Microwave the green beans for 1 minute.
3) Grease a skillet and heat over medium flame.
4) Sauté the mushrooms, onions, and garlic for 5 minutes.
5) In a bowl, combine the mushroom mixture and microwaved beans. Allow to cool.
6) In another bowl, mix the Greek yogurt, sour cream, salt, pepper, and cheddar cheese. Add into the mushroom and bean mixture.
7) Toss and place in a baking dish.
8) Bake for 25 minutes.

Nutrition Information:
Calories per serving: 107; Protein: 8.4g; Carbs: 14.5g; Fat: 2.2g Sugar: 4.5g

Mexican Bell Pepper Casserole

Serves: 4
Cooking Time: 35 minutes

Ingredients:
3 large eggs
12 ounces low fat plain Greek yogurt
Salt and pepper to taste
1 teaspoon cumin
½ teaspoon coriander
½ teaspoon dry mustard
1 teaspoon olive oil
½ cup thinly sliced onions
1 clove garlic, minced
2 cups chopped bell peppers
8 ounces reduced fat cheddar cheese

Directions:
1) Preheat the oven to 375°F.
2) Beat the eggs and yogurt in a bowl until fluffy. Season with salt, pepper, cumin, coriander, and dry mustard. Set aside.
3) In a medium skillet, heat oil over medium flame. Sauté the onions and garlic for 30 seconds.
4) Spread the sauteed garlic and onions in a casserole dish. Pour in the beaten eggs over the garlic. Add in the bell peppers and top with cheddar cheese.
5) Bake in the oven for 30 minutes.

Nutrition Information:
Calories per serving: 221; Protein: 14.9g; Carbs: 16.2g; Fat: 11.1g Sugar:8.8 g

Tofu Power Bowl

Serves: 1
Cooking Time: 10 minutes

Ingredients:
15 ounces extra firm tofu
2 tablespoons soy sauce
1 teaspoon rice vinegar
1 teaspoon sesame oil
½ cup cubed eggplant
½ cup grated cauliflower
½ cup chopped kale

Directions:
1) Press the tofu in a clean paper towel to remove excess liquid. Slice into strips.
2) In a bowl, combine the soy sauce and vinegar. Set aside.
3) Heat the sesame oil in a skillet over medium flame and cook the cubed tofu and eggplants until golden brown on all sides. Set aside.
4) Cook the cauliflower and kale separately.
5) Assemble the bowl by putting the vegetables in a bowl. Top with the tofu.
6) Drizzle with the sauce.

Nutrition Information:
Calories per serving: 548; Protein: 46.1g; Carbs: 22.3g; Fat: 35.6g Sugar: 10.6g

Rosemary Cauliflower Rolls

Serves: 4
Cooking Time: 30 minutes

Ingredients:
4 cups riced cauliflower
1/3 cup almond flour
2 eggs, beaten
1/3 cup reduced fat shredded mozzarella cheese
2 tablespoons fresh rosemary, chopped
Salt to taste

Directions:
1) Preheat the oven to 400°F.
2) Combine all ingredients in a bowl and mix everything.
3) Scoop the cauliflower mixture into evenly sized biscuits.
4) Place on a foil-lined baking sheet.
5) Place in the oven and bake for 30 minutes until golden brown.

Nutrition Information:
Calories per serving: 106; Protein: 9.5g; Carbs: 6.4g; Fat: 5.2g Sugar: 2.5g

Cauliflower Bread Sticks

Serves: 1
Cooking Time: 40 minutes

Ingredients:
1 cup raw grated cauliflower
¼ cup egg whites
1 cup 2% light mozzarella cheese, shredded
¼ cup Italian seasoning
Salt and pepper to taste

Directions:
1) Preheat the oven to 350°F.
2) Place all ingredients in a bowl. Mix until well-combined.
3) Spread the mixture evenly into a pan and bake for 30 minutes until golden brown.
4) Allow to cool before slicing into sticks.
5) Place in a foil-lined baking sheet and bake the cauliflower sticks for another 10 minutes.

Nutrition Information:
Calories per serving: 346; Protein: 46.9g; Carbs: 33.8g; Fat: 0.5g Sugar: 10.2g

Italian Zucchini Bake

Serves: 4
Cooking Time: 35 minutes

Ingredients:
10 ounces 93% lean ground beef
1 cup canned Italian diced tomatoes
¼ teaspoon garlic powder
1/8 teaspoon salt
1/8 teaspoon pepper
4 ounces part-skim ricotta
6 ounces reduced fat mozzarella cheese
3 tablespoons reduced fat parmesan cheese
¼ teaspoon Italian seasoning
1 large zucchini, sliced into thin circles

Directions:
1) Preheat the oven to 350°F.
2) Heat skillet over medium flame and add the ground beef. Sauté for 5 minutes until golden. Add in the tomatoes, garlic powder, salt and pepper. Cook for another 3 minutes. Set aside.
3) In a bowl, combine the ricotta, mozzarella, parmesan, and Italian seasoning.
4) In a baking dish, layer the ground beef, cheese mixture, and zucchini.
5) Place in the oven for 30 minutes.

Nutrition Information:
Calories per serving:266; Protein: 36.6g; Carbs: 4.1g; Fat: 3.2g Sugar: 1.2g

Zucchini Fritters

Serves: 4
Cooking Time: 30 minutes

Ingredients:
1 large zucchini, sliced
1 clove garlic, minced
¼ cup fresh basil
¼ cup fresh oregano
2 organic eggs, beaten
2 tablespoons almond flour
¼ teaspoon onion powder
½ teaspoon salt
¼ teaspoon pepper

Directions:
1) Preheat the oven to 350°F.
2) Mix all ingredients in a bowl and toss to coat the zucchini with the seasoning.
3) Place the coated zucchini in a baking sheet lined with foil.
4) Place in the oven and bake for 30 minutes until crisp.

Nutrition Information:
Calories per serving: 72; Protein: 4.9g; Carbs: 1.4g; Fat: 5.2g Sugar: 0.5g

Loaded Cauliflower Soup

Serves: 4
Cooking Time: 15 minutes

Ingredients:
1 teaspoon olive oil
¼ cup diced onion
½ cup diced celery
2 cloves garlic, minced
4 cups chopped cauliflower florets
1 medium zucchini, chopped
2 cups vegetable broth
1 bay leaf
¼ teaspoon salt and pepper
1 5 ounces low fat plain Greek yogurt
1 ½ cups reduced fat shredded cheddar cheese
Chives for garnish

Directions:
1) Heat oil in a skillet over medium flame. Sauté the onions, celery, and garlic for a minute until fragrant.
2) Stir in the rest of the ingredients.
3) Close the lid and allow to simmer for 10 minutes.
4) Serve immediately.

Nutrition Information:
Calories per serving: 152; Protein: 16.3g; Carbs: 10.4g; Fat: 5.5g Sugar: 5.3g

Caprese Salad

Serves: 4
Cooking Time: 5 minutes

Ingredients:
4 ounces fresh reduced fat mozzarella cheese, cubed
1 cup baby spinach
1 cup roma tomatoes, sliced
¼ cup chopped fresh basil
1/8 teaspoon salt
1/8 teaspoon pepper
2 tablespoons balsamic vinegar

Directions:
1) Place the vegetables in a bowl.
2) In another bowl, mix together salt, pepper, and balsamic vinegar.
3) Drizzle over the salad.
4) Toss to coat.

Nutrition Information:
Calories per serving: 50; Protein: 9.4g; Carbs: 2.9g; Fat: 0.01g Sugar: 1.8g

Balsamic Mushroom Kabobs

Serves: 4
Cooking Time:10 minutes

Ingredients:
4 cups mushrooms
2 tablespoons balsamic vinegar
1 tablespoon soy sauce
3 cloves garlic, minced
½ teaspoon thyme
¼ teaspoon salt
¼ teaspoon pepper

Directions:
1) Combine all ingredients in a Ziploc bag.
2) Close and allow to marinate in the fridge for at least 3 hours.
3) Skewer the mushrooms and cook in a grill over medium heat for 3 minutes per side.

Nutrition Information:
Calories per serving: 44; Protein: 3.5g; Carbs: 6.5g; Fat: 1.1g Sugar: 4g

Ranch Broccoli Slaw

Serves: 2
Cooking Time: 5 minutes

Ingredients:
1 ½ cups broccoli florets, chopped
1 tablespoon reduced fat buttermilk ranch dressing
¼ cup reduced fat cheddar cheese, shredded
1 tablespoon turkey bacon bits, fried and chopped (optional)

Directions:

1) Combine all ingredients in a bowl. Stir until well combined.
2) Chill in the fridge before serving.

Nutrition Information:
Calories per serving:84; Protein: 8.4g; Carbs: 8.7g; Fat: 2.5g Sugar: 2g

Cauliflower Tortillas

Serves: 2
Cooking Time: 20 minutes

Ingredients:
2 cups riced cauliflower
½ cup liquid egg substitute
2/3 cup part-skim shredded mozzarella cheese
1 teaspoon low sodium seasoning

Directions:
1) Preheat the oven to 425ºF.
2) Combine all ingredients in a bowl. Mix until well-combined.
3) Place cauliflower mixture in parchment paper and flatten to create a tortilla.
4) Bake for 15 minutes until the edges becomes crispy.

Nutrition Information:
Calories per serving:173; Protein: 17.5g; Carbs: 11.4g; Fat: 6.9g Sugar: 4.1g

Spinach Quiche

Serves: 2
Cooking Time: minutes

Ingredients:
3 eggs, beaten
½ cup white mushrooms, sliced thinly
½ cup red bell pepper, diced
1 cup raw spinach
½ cup reduced-fat shredded mozzarella cheese
Cooking spray
Salt and pepper to taste

Directions:
1) Preheat the oven to 350°F.
2) Combine all ingredients in a bowl. Pour mixture in a pie plate.
3) Bake for 30 minutes or until the edges turn golden.

Nutrition Information:
Calories per serving: 290; Protein: 21.5g; Carbs: 6.3g; Fat: 20g Sugar: 2.9g

Healthy Express Chow Mein

Serves: 5
Cooking Time: 5 minutes

Ingredients:
1 teaspoon olive oil
4 cloves garlic, minced
1 ½ teaspoon grated ginger
1 cup celery, chopped
4 cups zucchini noodles
¼ cup low sodium soy sauce
2 teaspoons toasted sesame oil
½ cup green onion, chopped
2 cups shredded cabbaged
½ teaspoon salt

Directions:

1) Heat the oil in a skillet over medium flame and sauté the garlic, ginger, and celery until fragrant.
2) Stir in the zucchini noodles and season with soy sauce. Stir for 2 minutes before adding the sesame oil, onion, and cabbage. Season with salt.
3) Continue stirring for another 3 minutes until the vegetables are wilted.

Nutrition Information:
Calories per serving: 236; Protein: 7.8g; Carbs: 44g; Fat: 3.1g Sugar: 2g

Veggie Quesadilla

Serves: 1
Cooking Time:40 minutes

Ingredients:
1 cup cooked spaghetti squash meat
¼ cup egg beaters
3/8 cup reduced fat shredded Mexican cheese
1/8 teaspoon garlic powder
1/8 teaspoon onion powder
1/8 teaspoon pepper
¼ teaspoon whole oregano leaves, crushed
½ cup reduced fat shredded Mexican cheese
¼ cup canned green chilies, chopped
¼ cup chopped mushrooms
2 tablespoons salsa

Directions:
1) Preheat the oven to 425°F.
2) In a bowl, combine the spaghetti squash meat, egg beaters, Mexican cheese, garlic powder, onion powder, pepper, and oregano leaves.
3) Press the mixture in a parchment-lined baking sheet as thin as possible. Bake for 30 minutes. Bake for 30 minutes.
4) Spread ¼ of the cheese over half of the baked tortilla.
5) Spread he chilies and mushrooms over the cheese. Top with the remaining ¼ cup of the cheese.
6) Fold the tortilla and bake for 7 more minutes.
7) Serve with salsa.

Nutrition Information:
Calories per serving: 344; Protein: 36.8g; Carbs: 21.6g; Fat: 5.7g Sugar: 7.1g

Zucchini Noodles with Avocado Pesto

Serves: 4
Cooking Time: 5 minutes

Ingredients:
6 cups spiralized zucchinis
1 tablespoon olive oil
6-ounce avocado, meat scooped
1 cup basil leaves
3 cups garlic cloves
1/3-ounce pine nuts
2 tablespoons lemon juice
½ teaspoon salt
¼ teaspoon black pepper

Directions:
1) Place the spiralized zucchini on a bowl lined with paper towel to draw up excess water. Remove and place on a bowl.
2) In a food processor, place the remaining ingredients and pulse until smooth.
3) Pour the avocado pesto over the zucchini and mix until the zucchini noodles are coated with the pesto sauce.

Nutrition Information:
Calories per serving: 271; Protein: 8.2g; Carbs: 38.8g; Fat: 5.4g Sugar: 1.8g

Cauliflower Alfredo Sauce

Serves: 6
Cooking Time: 10 minutes

Ingredients:
1 tablespoon olive oil
1 tablespoon garlic, minced
3 cups cauliflower florets
1 ½ cups water
1 ½ cups low sodium vegetable broth
½ teaspoon salt
¼ teaspoon black pepper
¼ cup unsweetened almond milk
1 tablespoon parmesan cheese

Directions:
1) Heat the olive oil in a skillet over medium flame. Sauté the garlic for 30 seconds before adding the cauliflower.
2) Add in the water, broth, salt, and pepper. Bring to a boil for 10 minutes
3) Drain the cauliflower but reserve ½ cup of the broth used to boil it.
4) To a food processor, add in the cooked cauliflower, ½ cup of reserved broth, and milk. Season with more salt and pepper to taste.
5) Pulse until smooth.
6) Serve with zucchini noodles and top with parmesan cheese.

Nutrition Information:
Calories per serving: 56; Protein: 2g; Carbs: 6g; Fat: 1g; Sugar: 0.7g

Lean and Green Chicken, Turkey, Beef, Pork, and Game Meat Recipes

Chicken Asparagus Risotto

Serves: 4
Cooking Time: 30 minutes

Ingredients:
2 pounds boneless skinless chicken breasts
¼ teaspoon salt
¼ teaspoon pepper
2 tablespoons butter
1 ¼ pounds grated cauliflower
¼ pounds asparagus, chopped
½ cup chicken stock
4 tablespoons nutritional yeast

Directions:
1) Preheat the oven to 350°F.
2) Place the chicken in a dish and season with salt and pepper to taste. Pour butter on top of the chicken and bake in the oven for 30 minutes. Remove from the oven and allow to rest.
3) In a skillet, combine the cauliflower and asparagus. Add chicken stock and simmer for 10 minutes until tender.
4) When finished place chicken on top and garnish with nutritional yeast.

Nutrition Information:
Calories per serving: 409; Protein: 59.9g; Carbs: 13.2g; Fat: 12.6g Sugar: 4.2g

Mediterranean Chicken Salad

Serves: 2
Cooking Time: 25 minutes

Ingredients:
1 ¾ pounds boneless chicken breasts
1 ½ tablespoon butter, melted
¼ teaspoon salt
¼ tablespoon pepper
6 cups romaine lettuce, torn
1 cup sliced cucumber
1-pint cherry tomatoes, halved
10 pitted kalamata olives
1/3 cup reduced-fat feta cheese
1 small lemon, juiced

Directions:
1) Preheat the oven to 350°F.
2) Season the chicken with butter, salt, and black pepper
3) Grill the chicken for 25 minutes or until the interna temperature reaches to 165°F.
4) Allow the chicken to rest before slicing.
5) While the chicken is resting, mix the remaining ingredients in a bowl. Toss to coat.
6) Serve chicken on top.

Nutrition Information:
Calories per serving: 372; Protein: 75g; Carbs:9.1 g; Fat: 6.8g Sugar: 2.1g

Baked Chipotle Chicken

Serves: 4
Cooking Time: 30 minutes

Ingredients:
1 14 ounces can fire-roasted tomatoes, diced
1 canned chipotle pepper in adobo sauce
1 teaspoon cumin
½ teaspoon dried oregano
¼ teaspoon salt
1 ½ pounds boneless chicken breasts
1 cup reduced-fat shredded Mexican cheese blend

Directions:
1) Preheat the oven to 400°F.
2) Combine the tomatoes, chipotle pepper, cumin, oregano, and salt in a food processor. Pulse until smooth. Set aside.
3) Place the chicken breasts in a heat-proof dish. Pour over the sauce.
4) Place in the oven and bake for 30 minutes.
5) Five minutes before the cooking time ends, sprinkle with cheese.

Nutrition Information:
Calories per serving: 306; Protein: 46.3g; Carbs: 5.8g; Fat: 10.3g Sugar: 3.2g

Sheet Pan Chicken Lettuce Wraps

Serves: 4
Cooking Time: 30 minutes

Ingredients:
1-pound chicken breasts, sliced into thick strips
2 bell peppers, julienned
2 teaspoons olive oil
2 teaspoons fajita seasoning
Juice from ½ lime
6 leaves romaine lettuce

Directions:
1) Preheat the oven to 400°F.
2) Combine all ingredients except for the lettuce wraps in a Ziploc bag. Allow to marinate in the fridge for an hour.
3) Spread the contents of the bag on a foil-lined baking sheet.
4) Bake for 30 minutes.
5) Serve on lettuce leaves.

Nutrition Information:
Calories per serving: 237; Protein: 24.7g; Carbs: 4.8g; Fat: 12.9g Sugar: 1.9g

Mongolian Beef Over Cauliflower Rice

Serves: 4
Cooking Time: 10 minutes

Ingredients:
Cooking spray
2 cloves garlic, minced
1 cup diced scallions
½ teaspoon ginger, minced
1 ½ pounds flank steak, thinly sliced
2 cups broccoli florets
½ cup chicken broth
1/3 cup reduced sodium soy sauce
4 cups cauliflower rice, blanched

Directions:
1) Heat cooking oil over medium flame and sauté the garlic and scallions for 1 minute until wilted.
2) Stir in the ginger and flank steak. Stir for 3 minutes.
3) Add the broccoli, broth, and season with soy sauce.
4) Close the lid and simmer for 6 minutes.
5) Serve with cauliflower rice.

Nutrition Information:
Calories per serving: 383; Protein: 47.8g; Carbs: 13.7g; Fat: 4.8g Sugar: 3g

Cheesy Chicken Cauliflower Chicken Skillet

Serves: 4
Cooking Time: 15 minutes

Ingredients:
2 tablespoons olive oil
2 cloves garlic, minced
2 pounds chicken breasts, chopped
½ cup chicken broth
1 ½ cups sliced mushrooms
1 12 ounces cauliflower florets
8 ounces reduced fat shredded mozzarella cheese
½ teaspoons dried oregano
2 scallions, chopped

Directions:
1) Heat the oil in skillet over medium flame.
2) Sauté the garlic for 30 seconds until fragrant.
3) Stir in the chicken broth and mushrooms. Bring to a simmer for 10 minutes.
4) Add the cauliflower, mozzarella, oregano, and scallions.
5) Season with salt and pepper to taste.
6) Cook for another 3 minutes

Nutrition Information:
Calories per serving: 504; Protein: 53.7g; Carbs: 10.4g; Fat: 20.1g Sugar: 2.7g

Instant Pot BBQ Pulled Pork with Greek Yogurt Slaw

Serves: 4
Cooking Time: 60 minutes

Ingredients:
1 ½ pounds pork tenderloin, cut in half
1 12 ounce can diet root beer
3 cups shredded cabbage
½ cup plain low-fat Greek yogurt
1 tablespoon apple cider vinegar
2 teaspoons lemon juice
1 teaspoon Dijon mustard
¼ teaspoon celery salt
½ cup sugar-free barbecue sauce

Directions:
1) Place pork in Instant Pot and press the Sauté button. Sauté the pork for 3 minutes until browned. Add in the root beer.
2) Close the lid and set the vent to the Sealing position. Press the Manual button and adjust the cooking time to 60 minutes.
3) Meanwhile, prepare the slaw by mixing in a bowl the cabbage, Greek yogurt, vinegar, lemon juice, Dijon mustard, and salt.
4) Once the pork is cooked, remove from the Instant Pot and shred using forks. Add barbecue sauce and toss to combine.
5) Serve pulled pork with cabbage slaw.

Nutrition Information:
Calories per serving: 321; Protein: 47.3g; Carbs: 16.5g; Fat: 6.6g Sugar: 14g

Cheeseburger Pie

Serves: 4
Cooking Time: 1 hour and 10 minutes

Ingredients:
1 large spaghetti squash
1-pound lean ground beef
¼ cups diced onion
2 eggs, beaten
2 tablespoons tomato paste
½ teaspoon Worcestershire sauce
2/3 cup reduced fat shredded cheddar cheese
2 ounces dill pickle slices

Directions:
1) Preheat the oven to 400°F.
2) Cut the spaghetti squash lengthwise and remove the seeds and pulp. Spray the insides with cooking spray and place the squash halves cut side down in a foil-lined baking sheet. Bake for 30 minutes. Once cooked, scrape the squash flesh with fork and set aside.
3) Press the squash meat into a greased pie pan. Create an even layer.
4) Prepare the meat filling by heating skillet over medium flame. Sauté the beef for 30 seconds then add the onion. Stir for 5 minutes. Drain and remove from heat.
5) In a bowl, whisk the eggs, yogurt, tomato paste, and Worcestershire sauce. Add in the ground beef. Mix until well combined.
6) Pour ground beef mixture into the spaghetti squash.
7) Bake for 40 minutes.
8) Garnish with pickles.

Nutrition Information:
Calories per serving: 365; Protein: 40.7g; Carbs: 5.3g; Fat: 9.1g Sugar: 2.6g

Mini Mac in A Bowl

Serves: 1
Cooking Time: minutes

Ingredients:

2 tablespoons diced yellow onion
5 ounces 99% lean ground beef
2 tablespoons light thousand island dressing
1/8 teaspoon white vinegar
1/8 teaspoon onion powder
3 cups shredded romaine lettuce
2 tablespoons reduced fat cheddar cheese
1 teaspoon sesame seeds

Directions:

1) Heat a skillet over medium flame. Grease skillet with cooking spray.
2) Add the onion and sauté for 1 minute. Add the beef and cook until lightly browned.
3) Meanwhile, mix the island dressing, white vinegar, and onion powder. Set aside.
4) Assemble by topping the lettuce with ground beef. Sprinkle cheese on top and garnish with pickle slices, and sesame seeds. Drizzle with sauce.

Nutrition Information:

Calories per serving: 416; Protein: 40.8g; Carbs: 14.5g; Fat: 14.1g Sugar: 7.9g

Philly Cheesesteak Stuffed Peppers

Serves: 4
Cooking Time: 60 minutes

Ingredients:

4 medium green bell peppers, sliced on top and seeded
1/3 cup diced yellow onion
2 cloves garlic, minced
¼ cup low sodium been broth
6 ounces baby Bella mushrooms, sliced
1-pound shaved deli roast beef
4 tablespoons low fat cream cheese
4 ounces reduced fat provolone cheese

Directions:

1) Preheat the oven to 400°F.
2) Set aside the bell pepper and make sure that they are clean inside.
3) In a skillet, sauté the onion and garlic in broth over medium flame for 5 minutes. Add the mushrooms and deli beef. Stir to cook everything.
4) Remove from skillet and stir in the cream cheese.
5) Line each of the bell pepper with a quarter slice of cheese Fill an eighth with the roast beef mixture and top with cheese.
6) Place in the oven and bake for 20 minutes.

Nutrition Information:

Calories per serving: 486; Protein: 43.7g; Carbs: 43.7g; Fat: 19g Sugar: 7.8g

Pesto Zucchini Noodles with Grilled Chicken

Serves: 4
Cooking Time: 5 minutes

Ingredients:
1/3 cup reduced fat Italian salad dressing
½ cup chopped fresh basil
½ cup parmesan cheese, divided
1/3 ounces pine nuts
Cooking spray
2 medium zucchinis, spiralized
1 ½ pounds grilled boneless chicken breasts, cubed
2 cups cherry tomatoes, halved
½ teaspoon crushed red pepper flakes

Directions:
1) Combine the salad dressing, basil, half of the parmesan cheese, and pine nuts. Pulse in a blender until smooth.
2) In a lightly greased skillet heated over medium flame, cook the zucchini noodles for 3 minutes. Stir in the pesto and remaining parmesan cheese.
3) Remove from heat and top with chicken, tomatoes, and crushed red pepper flakes.

Nutrition Information:
Calories per serving: 335; Protein: 43.5g; Carbs: 16.4g; Fat: 10.3g Sugar: 11.1g

Baked Chicken and Zucchini Casserole

Serves: 4
Cooking Time: 30 minutes

Ingredients:
1 ¾ pounds boneless chicken breasts
¼ teaspoon garlic powder
¼ teaspoon salt
¼ teaspoon pepper
4 teaspoons olive oil
1 cup diced zucchini
1 cup diced tomatoes
1 teaspoon basil leaves
1 teaspoon oregano
1 cup part-skim mozzarella cheese

Directions:
1) Butterfly the chicken slices in half to make four thin pieces.
2) Season with garlic powder, salt and pepper.
3) Heat skillet over medium flame and add oil.
4) Brown the chicken slices in olive oil for 3 minutes on each side. Place the chicken in a baking dish. Set aside.
5) To the same skillet, sauté the zucchini in pan until soft then add the tomatoes, basil and oregano. Season with more salt and pepper to taste.
6) Pour vegetable over chicken and top with mozzarella cheese.
7) Bake for 20 minutes in a 350°F preheated oven.

Nutrition Information:
Calories per serving: 373; Protein: 52.3g; Carbs: 5.3g; Fat: 14.7g Sugar: 1.3g

Arroz Con Pollo

Serves: 4
Cooking Time: 30 minutes

Ingredients:
1 ¾ pounds boneless chicken breasts
¼ teaspoon salt and pepper
2 cloves of garlic, minced
1 scallion, minced
4 cups cauliflower, grated
1 ½ cups cherry tomatoes, halved
40 green olives, pitted
½ cup green beans, cut into ¼ inch pieces

Directions:
1) Preheat the oven to 350°F.
2) Season the chicken with salt and pepper. Place on aa greased baking sheet.
3) Roast the chicken for 20 minutes. Remove from the oven and set aside.
4) Meanwhile, mix all ingredients in a pot and simmer on low for 10 minutes.
5) Serve the cauliflower rice with the chicken.

Nutrition Information:
Calories per serving: 314; Protein: 47.4g; Carbs: 8.4g; Fat: 9.7g Sugar: 2.9g

Mexican Turkey Soup

Serves: 10
Cooking Time: 30 minutes

Ingredients:
¼ cup olive oil
1 jalapeno, seeds removed then chopped
1 cup cilantro, chopped
2 cups green onions, finely chopped
3 cloves of garlic, minced
1 cup red bell pepper, seeded and chopped
1 teaspoon dried oregano
½ teaspoon cayenne pepper
Salt and pepper to taste
12 ounces turkey breast, sliced
6 roma tomatoes, chopped
2 cups chicken stock
2 cups tomato sauce

Directions:
1) Heat oil in a large pot and add the jalapeno, green onion, cilantro, garlic, bell pepper, oregano, cayenne pepper. Season with salt and pepper to taste. Cook for 10 minutes on low heat.
2) Add the turkey and cook for another 3 minutes before stirring in the tomatoes.
3) Add the remaining ingredients.
4) Bring to a boil for 10 minutes.
5) Remove from the heat and serve.

Nutrition Information:
Calories per serving: 427; Protein: 52.7g; Carbs: 15.9g; Fat: 10.2g Sugar:8.9g

Bibimbap Bowls

Serves: 4
Cooking Time: 15 minutes

Ingredients:
1 teaspoon olive oil
5 cups baby spinach
1 teaspoon toasted sesame oil
¼ teaspoon salt
1 pound 98% lean ground beef
2 tablespoons chili garlic sauce
1 tablespoon reduced sodium soy sauce
2 cups cauliflower, grated
1 cup sliced cucumber
4 fried eggs
½ cups green onions
1 tablespoon sesame seeds

Directions:
1) Heat the oil in a skillet over medium flame. Add the spinach and cook until wilted. Drizzle with sesame seed oil and season with salt. Remove spinach and set aside.
2) Using the same pan, add the beef and cook for 6 minutes while stirring constantly until golden brown. Add the chili garlic sauce and soy sauce and cook for another minute. Remove from heat.
3) Place cauliflower in a microwavable container and heat for 3 minutes until tender.
4) Assemble the bibimbap. Divide the cauliflower rice in 4 containers. Distribute with spinach, beef, cucumber and egg.
5) Garnish with green onions and sesame seeds.

Nutrition Information:
Calories per serving: 410; Protein: 39.5g; Carbs: 12.8g; Fat: 8.7g Sugar: 3.4g

Cauliflower and Chicken Tzatziki Bowl

Serves: 4
Cooking Time: 30 minutes

Ingredients:

5 ½ cups riced cauliflower
1 tablespoons parmesan cheese
¼ teaspoon salt, divided
1-pound boneless chicken breasts, cut into strips
½ cup grated cucumber
½ cup low-fat Greek yogurt, plain
½ cup crushed garlic

Directions:

1) Mix together the cauliflower rice, parmesan cheese, and salt. Place in a microwave oven and cook for 1 minute. Set aside.
2) Preheat the oven to 425°F. Season the chicken with salt and bake in the oven for 30 minutes or until golden brown.
3) Meanwhile, place the cucumber, yogurt, and garlic in a bowl. Season with salt and mix until well combined.
4) Assemble by putting the cauliflower rice in a bowl. Prepare four bowls. Top with baked chicken and drizzle with the tzatziki sauce.

Nutrition Information:

Calories per serving: 283; Protein: 29.6g; Carbs: 15.6g; Fat: 8.8g Sugar: 5.3g

Turkey Meatball and Squash Noodle Soup

Serves: 5
Cooking Time: 25 minutes

Ingredients:
1 ½ pounds 93% lean ground turkey
½ cup low-fat grated parmesan cheese
2 scallions, trimmed and minced
1 teaspoon salt
½ teaspoon black pepper
4 cups chicken stock
2 tablespoons nonpareil capers
4 cups zucchini, spiralized into noodles
2 cups cherry tomatoes, halved
1 cup chopped fresh basil

Directions:
1) In a bowl, combine the turkey and cheese. Add the scallions, half of the salt, and pepper. Mix until well-combined. Form 12 small meatballs and set aside in the fridge to set.
2) Bring the chicken stock to a rolling boil and bring the temperature down to a simmer. Add the turkey meatballs, capers and simmer for 15 minutes.
3) Add in the zucchini noodles, tomatoes, and basil. Cook for another 5 minutes.
4) Serve immediately.

Nutrition Information:
Calories per serving: 400; Protein: 42g; Carbs: 15g; Fat: 15g Sugar: 3g

Pesto Zucchini Noodles with Grilled Chicken

Serves: 4
Cooking Time: 10 minutes

Ingredients:
1/3 cup reduced fat Italian salad dressing
¼ cup chopped fresh basil
½ cup parmesan cheese, divided
1/3-ounce pine nuts
2 large zucchinis, spiralized
1 ½ pounds grilled boneless chicken breasts, sliced into strips
2 cups cherry tomatoes
½ teaspoon crushed red pepper flakes

Directions:
1) Combine the salad dressing, basil, half of the parmesan cheese, and pine nuts in a food processor. Blend until smooth.
2) Grease the skillet over medium heat and cook the zucchini noodles until tender. Stir in the pesto and cook for 3 minutes.
3) Plate the zucchini noodles and top with grilled chicken, tomatoes, and red pepper flakes.

Nutrition Information:
Calories per serving: 335; Protein: 43.5g; Carbs: 16.4g; Fat: 10.3g Sugar: 4g

Chicken Cobb Salad

Serves: 2
Cooking Time: 5 minutes

Ingredients:

4 cups romaine lettuce, torn
½ pound cooked chicken breasts, cubed
2 hard-boiled eggs, sliced
1 cup cherry tomatoes, halved
2 slices cooked turkey bacon, chopped
¼ cup non-fat, plain yogurt
¼ avocado, mashed
3 tablespoons reduced sodium ranch dressing

Directions:

1) Place lettuce in a salad bowl and top with chicken, eggs, tomatoes, and turkey bacon.
2) In another bowl, mix together the remaining ingredients.
3) Drizzle over the salad.
4) Serve immediately.

Nutrition Information:

Calories per serving: 525; Protein: 50g; Carbs: 17.7g; Fat: 12g Sugar: 11.7g

Meat Stew with Cauliflower

Serves: 4
Cooking Time: 1 hour and 5 minutes

Ingredients:

½ teaspoon salt
¼ teaspoon pepper
½ teaspoon onion powder
1 ½ pounds boneless chuck roast, fat trimmed and cut into chunks
1 8 ounces package sliced baby Bella mushrooms
3 cups low-sodium chicken broth, divided
2 teaspoon Dijon mustard
2 teaspoon balsamic vinegar
1 tablespoon sugar-free maple syrup
1 teaspoon thyme
2 cloves of garlic, minced
16 ounces cauliflower florets

Directions:

1) Rub salt, pepper, and onion powder onto the roast and place in the slow cooker. Add the mushrooms, chicken broth, Dijon mustard, balsamic vinegar, maple syrup, thyme, and garlic.
2) Close the lid and set the vent to the Sealing position. Press the manual button and adjust the cooking time to 60 minutes.
3) Do quick pressure release to open the lid and add the cauliflowers.
4) Close the lid and Set the button to the Sauté function. Cook for another 5 minutes.

Nutrition Information:

Calories per serving: 391; Protein: 53.2g; Carbs: 16.2g; Fat: 10.2g Sugar: 4.2g

Steak with Mushroom Shallot Sauce

Serves: 4
Cooking Time: 10 minutes

Ingredients:
1 ½ pounds sirloin steak, 1-inch thick
¼ teaspoon salt
½ teaspoon black pepper
Olive oil pan spray
2 teaspoons Dijon mustard
2 teaspoons red wine vinegar
2 tablespoons shallots, chopped
18 ounces green beans, trimmed and blanched

Directions:

1) Season the steak with salt and pepper.
2) Heat oil in skillet over medium high heat and cook steak on each side for 5 minutes. Allow to rest for 5 minutes before slicing against the grain.
3) In a bowl, combine the mustard and wine vinegar. Add the shallots.
4) Top steak with mustard sauce and serve with green beans

Nutrition Information:
Calories per serving: 356; Protein: 36.9g; Carbs: 6.7g; Fat: 19.6g Sugar: 1.4g

Tomatillo and Green Chili Pork Stew

Serves: 4
Cooking Time: 40 minutes

Ingredients:
2 cloves garlic, minced
2 scallions, chopped
1-pound tomatillos, chopped
2 serrano chilies, seeded and chopped
½ teaspoon dried oregano
8 large romaine lettuce leaves, torn
1 ½ pounds boneless pork loin, cubed
¼ teaspoon each salt and pepper
¼ cup cilantro, chopped
1 cup sliced radishes
4 lime wedges

Directions:
1) Place the garlic, scallions, tomatillos, chilies, and oregano in a blender. Add ½ of the lettuce. Pulse until smooth.
2) Place pork and tomatillo puree in a pot and add 1 cup of water. Season with salt and pepper to taste.
3) Close the lid and bring to a boil before reducing the heat to a simmer. Simmer for 30 minutes.
4) Add the lettuce and cook for another 2 minutes.
5) When the stew is cooked, garnish with cilantro, radishes and lime wedges.

Nutrition Information:
Calories per serving: 370; Protein: 36g; Carbs: 14g; Fat: 19g Sugar: 2g

Turkey Meatloaf with Fennel

Serves: 6
Cooking Time: 30 minutes

Ingredients:
2 pounds 99% lean ground turkey
3 cups finely chopped cabbage
2 green onions, minced
¼ cup pine nuts, toasted then crushed
1 teaspoon paprika
1 teaspoon salt, divided
1 teaspoon black pepper
1 tablespoon olive oil
2 small fennel bulbs, finely chopped
2/3 cup stock
2 tablespoons parmesan cheese

Directions:
1) Preheat the oven to 400°F.
2) In a bowl, combine all ingredients until well combined.
3) Place in a loaf pan lined with parchment paper and press over the mold.
4) Bake for 30 minutes.

Nutrition Information:
Calories per serving: 400; Protein: 61g; Carbs: 14g; Fat: 18g Sugar: 3g

Grilled Fajita Bowls

Serves: 4
Cooking Time: 20 minutes

Ingredients:
1 1/4 pounds flank steak
1 teaspoon ground cumin
1 teaspoon chili powder
1/4 teaspoon each salt and pepper
2 scallions, whole
1 lime, cut in half
8 cups lettuce, torn
1 bell pepper, seeded and halved
1 cup diced tomatoes
1 jalapeno, sliced
1 cup cilantro, chopped
1/4 cup sour cream

Directions:
1) Heat the grill.
2) In a bowl, place the steak and add the cumin, chili powder, salt, and pepper. Rub the mixture all over the steak.
3) Grill the steak on both sides until the internal temperature reaches 145°F.
4) Remove from heat and allow to rest before slicing.
5) Grill the scallions for 3 minutes. Chop then set aside.
6) Assemble the fajita by add the beef, scallions, lettuce, lime, bell pepper, tomatoes, jalapenos, and cilantro.
7) Drizzle with sour cream.

Nutrition Information:
Calories per serving: 290; Protein: 32g; Carbs: 12g; Fat: 13g Sugar: 1g

Jerk Crusted Pork Chop

Serves:
Cooking Time: minutes

Ingredients:

4 bone-in pork chops
1 teaspoon lime juice
1 tablespoon jerk seasoning
¼ teaspoon salt, divided
8 ounces baby spinach
1 cup sliced radishes
1 cup fresh diced tomatoes
1 tablespoon lemon juice
½ teaspoon ground black pepper.

Directions:

1) Season the pork chops with lime juice, jerk seasoning, and salt. Allow to marinate for 30 minutes.
2) Cook the pork chops in a broiler oven at 450°F for 10 minutes.
3) Meanwhile, heat 3 tablespoons of water in a pot and cook the spinach until wilted. Set aside.
4) Assemble by putting in a bowl the spinach, radishes, tomatoes, and pork. Drizzle with lemon juice and black pepper.

Nutrition Information:

Calories per serving: 300; Protein: 28g; Carbs: 12g; Fat: 16g Sugar:2 g

Fueling Recipes

Honey Mustard Chicken Nuggets

Serves: 2
Cooking Time: 20 minutes

Ingredients:
12 ounces boneless chicken breasts, cubed
1 egg, beaten
2 sachets Optavia Essential Honey Mustard & Onion Sticks, crushed
¼ cup low fat Greek yogurt
2 teaspoons spicy brown mustard
¼ teaspoon garlic powder
Cooking spray

Directions:
1) Preheat the oven to 400°F.
2) Place the chicken breasts in a bowl. Place egg and Optavia Honey Mustard & Onion Sticks in separate bowls.
3) Dip the chicken in egg then dredge in the crushed Optavia sticks until coated. Place chicken on a greased foil-lined baking sheet. Spray with cooking oil.
4) Bake in the oven for 20 minutes until golden. Make sure to flip halfway through the cooking time.
5) Meanwhile, combine the yogurt, mustard and garlic powder in a bowl.
6) Serve chicken with the dip.

Nutrition Information:
Calories per serving: 381; Protein: 41.8g; Carbs: 3.3g; Fat: 21.2g Sugar: 2.5g

Smashed Potato Grilled Cheese

Serves: 2
Cooking Time: 10 minutes

Ingredients:
2 sachets Optavia Essential Smashed Potatoes
1 cup water
1 cup reduced fat shredded cheese (mozzarella, cheddar, or pepper jack)

Directions:
1) In a microwave-safe bowl, mix the Optavia Smashed potatoes and water. Mix until well-combined.
2) Microwave for 1 ½ minutes then stir.
3) Pour the mixture in a greased waffle iron. Close the lid and cook for 12 minutes.
4) Open the lid and sprinkle cheese on half of the waffle. Fold the waffle over the cheese then close the waffle iron. Continue cooking for another 3 minutes.

Nutrition Information:
Calories per serving: 364; Protein: 25.3g; Carbs: 66.4g; Fat: 0.3g Sugar: 3.7g

Silky Peanut Butter Cookies

Serves: 4
Cooking Time: 12 minutes

Ingredients:
4 sachets Optavia Essential Silky Peanut Butter Shake
¼ teaspoon baking powder
¼ cup unsweetened almond milk
1 tablespoon softened butter
¼ teaspoon vanilla extract
1/8 teaspoon salt

Directions:
1) Preheat the oven to 350°F.
2) In a bowl, mix the Optavia Peanut Butter Shake and baking powder until well combined.
3) Add in the almond milk and butter. Stir in the vanilla extract. Mix until well combined.
4) Grease a baking sheet with cooking spray.
5) Use a cookie scoop and scoop out dough into small balls. Use fork to flatten the cookie dough and sprinkle with little salt on top.
6) Bake for 12 minutes.

Nutrition Information:
Calories per serving: 128; Protein: 4.8g; Carbs: 9g; Fat: 6.5g Sugar: 3g

Boo-Nila Shake

Serves: 1
Cooking Time: 5 minutes

Ingredients:
1 sachet Optavia Essential Creamy Vanilla Shake
8 ounces unsweetened almond milk
½ cup ice
2 tablespoons whipped topping

Directions:
1) Combine the first three ingredients in a blender. Pulse until smooth.
2) Pour into glass and top with whipped topping.

Nutrition Information:
Calories per serving: 258; Protein: 10.4g; Carbs: 29.5g; Fat: 10.7g Sugar: 18.8g

Buffalo Cauliflower Wings

Serves: 2
Cooking Time: 20 minutes

Ingredients:
2 sachets Optavia Select Buttermilk Cheddar Herb Biscuit
½ cup water
3 cups cauliflower florets
Cooking spray
¼ cup hot buffalo sauce
½ tablespoon melted butter
½ cup non-fat Greek yogurt, plain
1 teaspoon dry ranch dressing

Directions:

1) Preheat the oven to 425°F.
2) In a bowl, mix the Optavia Herb Biscuit with water until dissolved.
3) Add cauliflower florets and toss to coat with the breading.
4) Place cauliflower florets on a greased baking tray lined with foil.
5) Bake for 20 minutes.
6) Meanwhile, add the remaining ingredients in a bowl. Mix until combined.
7) Once the cauliflower is cooked, put in the bowl with the prepared mixture. Toss to coat.

Nutrition Information:
Calories per serving: 243; Protein: 12g; Carbs: 52.3g; Fat: 10.5g Sugar: 12g

Avocado on Toast

Serves: 1
Cooking Time: 5 minutes

Ingredients:
1 sachet Optavia Select Buttermilk Cheddar Herb Biscuit
1 ½ ounce avocado, mashed

Directions:
1) Bake Buttermilk Cheddar Herb Biscuit according to package directions.
2) Let cool and top with mashed avocado.

Nutrition Information:
Calories per serving: 233; Protein: 4.3g; Carbs: 28g; Fat: 11.9g Sugar: 4.5g

Sweet Potato Goat Cheese and Rosemary Quiche Cups

Serves: 3
Cooking Time: 35 minutes

Ingredients:
4 sachets Optavia Honey Sweet Potatoes
1 cup unsweetened almond milk
4 eggs, beaten
½ cup part-skimmed ricotta
1-ounce crumbled goat cheese
¼ cup diced yellow onions
1 tablespoon thyme
¼ teaspoon nutmeg
Cooking spray

Directions:

1) Preheat oven to 375°F.
2) In a microwavable safe bowl, mix the Optavia Sweet Potatoes and milk. Mix until combined. Microwave on high for 1 minute. Set aside.
3) Add remaining ingredients until well combined.
4) Place in a baking tray and cook in the oven for 35 minutes.

Nutrition Information:
Calories per serving: 349; Protein: 23.1g; Carbs: 11.2g; Fat: 23.2g Sugar: 7.7g

Peanut Butter Brownie Whoopie Pies

Serves: 2
Cooking Time: 20 minutes

Ingredients:
2 sachets Optavia Decadent Double Chocolate Brownie
¼ teaspoon baking powder
3 tablespoons liquid egg substitute
6 tablespoons unsweetened vanilla almond milk
1 teaspoon vegetable oil
¼ cup powdered peanut butter
Cooking spray

Directions:

1) Preheat oven to 350°F.
2) In a medium sized bowl, combine the Decadent Chocolate Brownie mixture, baking powder, egg substitute, half of the milk, and oil. Mix until a batter-like consistency is formed.
3) Divide the batter evenly among four slots of a light-greased muffin tin. Bake for 20 minutes or until a toothpick inserted in the middle comes out clean.
4) Meanwhile, combine the powdered peanut butter and the remaining milk.
5) Once cooled, slice each muffin in half and spread the peanut butter filling into the bottom half.

Nutrition Information:
Calories per serving: 210; Protein: 7.7g; Carbs: 21g; Fat:10 g Sugar: 9.3g

Cheesy Spinach Smashed Potatoes

Serves: 1
Cooking Time:5 minutes

Ingredients:

1 sachet Optavia Essential Roasted Garlic Creamy Smashed Potatoes
1 cup baby spinach
1 teaspoon water
½ cup reduced fat shredded mozzarella cheese
1 tablespoon grated Parmesan cheese

Directions:

1) Prepare Roasted Garlic Creamy Smashed Potatoes according to package instructions.
2) Steam spinach with water in the microwave for 1 minute.
3) Combine Roasted Garlic Creamy Smashed Potatoes, spinach, mozzarella, and parmesan cheese.

Nutrition Information:

Calories per serving: 398; Protein: 21g; Carbs: 52.6g; Fat:12 g Sugar: 0.4g

Chocolate Chip Funnel Cake Fries with Canola Dip

Serves: 2
Cooking Time: 5 minutes

Ingredients:
2 sachets Optavia Essential Golden Chocolate Chip Pancakes
¼ cup liquid egg substitute
2 teaspoons vegetable oil
¼ cup low fat plain Greek yogurt
2 tablespoons part-skim ricotta
2 packets zero-sugar substitute
½ teaspoon vanilla extract
A pinch of all spice

Directions:
1) In a bowl, combine the Golden Chocolate Chip Pancakes and egg substitute. Mix until a batter-like consistency is formed.
2) Pour batter in a resealable plastic bag and cut off a small part of one tip of the bag.
3) Heat oil in a medium-sized skillet over medium heat. Pipe the batter in long straight lines into skillet. Cook 1 to 2 minutes per side.
4) Meanwhile, prepare cannoli dip by mixing the remaining ingredients in a bowl.
5) Serve cake fries with cannoli dip.

Nutrition Information:
Calories per serving: 167; Protein: 7.1g; Carbs: 12.8g; Fat: 9.7g Sugar: 7,5g

Peanut Butter Brownie Whoopie Pies

Serves: 2
Cooking Time: 20 minutes

Ingredients:
2 sachets Optavia Decadent Double Chocolate Brownie
¼ teaspoon baking powder
3 tablespoons liquid egg substitute
6 tablespoons vanilla almond milk, unsweetened
1 teaspoon vegetable oil
¼ cup peanut butter
Cooking spray

Directions:
1) Preheat the oven to 350°F.
2) In a medium bowl, combine the Optavia Brownie mixture, baking powder, egg substitute, ¼ cup milk, and oil. Mix until a batter-like consistency is formed.
3) Divide the batter evenly in four lightly-greased muffin thin. Bake for 20 minutes until a toothpick inserted in the middle comes in.
4) Meanwhile, mix the powdered peanut butter and remaining milk.
5) Once cooled, slice each muffin in half horizontally. Spread one tablespoon of peanut butter filling into the bottom half of the brownie. Top with the remaining muffin halves.

Nutrition Information:
Calories per serving: 251; Protein: 6.7g; Carbs: 34.7g; Fat: 8.6g Sugar: 12.1g

Mini Cranberry Orange Spiced Cheesecake

Serves: 4
Cooking Time: 10 minutes

Ingredients:
4 Optavia Honey Chili Cranberry Nut Bars
1 ½ cups plain low-fat Greek yogurt
2 tablespoons sugar-free cheesecake flavored pudding mix
1 teaspoon orange zest

Directions:
1) Line a standard-sized muffin tin with eight cupcake liners.
2) Break each Honey Chili Cranberry Nut Bar in half. Place bar halves crunch-side down on a microwave-safe plate. Microwave for 20 to 30 seconds until softened. Place each half into the bottom of a cupcake liner and press to create a crust.
3) Repeat until the cupcake liners are filled.
4) In a large bowl, mix the Greek yogurt and pudding mix until well-combined.
5) Distribute the yogurt mixture among the cupcake liner and garnish the tops with orange zest.
6) Freeze for 30 minutes until solid.
7) Serve cold.

Nutrition Information:
Calories per serving: 236; Protein: 10.1g; Carbs: 16.5g; Fat: 12.3g Sugar: 7.2g

French Toast Sticks

Serves: 2
Cooking Time: 20 minutes

Ingredients:
2 sachets Optavia Essential Cinnamon Crunchy O's Cereal
2 tablespoons low-fate cream cheese, softened
6 tablespoons liquid egg substitute
Cooking spray
2 tablespoons, sugar-free syrup

Directions:
1) Process the Optavia Cereal in a food processor until a fine breadcrumb-like consistency is created.
2) Add the cream cheese and liquid egg substitute. Mix until a dough is formed.
3) Form six French toast stick pieces with the dough.
4) Heat a greased skillet over medium flame. Cook French toast sticks until warm and lightly browned.
5) Serve with the sugar-free syrup.

Nutrition Information:
Calories per serving: 170; Protein: 8.9g; Carbs: 27.9g; Fat: 3.3g Sugar: 12.8g

Blueberry Almond Breakfast Scones

Serves: 4
Cooking Time: 25 minutes

Ingredients:

4 sachets Optavia Blueberry Almond Hot Cereal
¼ cup ground flaxseed
1 packet zero-calorie sugar substitute
½ teaspoon baking powder
3 tablespoons unsalted butter, frozen and cut into cubes
3 tablespoons liquid egg white
3 tablespoons plain low-fat Greek yogurt
¼ teaspoon almond extract
¼ teaspoon cinnamon

Directions:

1) Preheat oven to 400°F.
2) Place the first four ingredients in a food processor. Pulse until well combined.
3) Add the frozen butter and pulse until the mixture becomes a coarse meal.
4) Add the egg white, Greek yogurt, milk, and almond extract and pulse until dough just comes together.
5) Form the dough into a six-inch circle onto a parchment-lined baking sheet. Sprinkle top with cinnamon.
6) Bake for 20 minutes until golden.
7) Once cooled, cut evenly into wedges.

Nutrition Information:

Calories per serving: 249; Protein: 5.4g; Carbs: 27.4g; Fat: 13.7g Sugar: 11g

Chocolate Peanut Butter Cups

Serves: 4
Cooking Time: 15 minutes

Ingredients:
¼ cup unsweetened almond milk
¼ cup plain low-fat Greek yogurt
A pinch of salt
4 packets stevia
¼ cup Optavia PB2 2
¼ cup + 1 tablespoon water
Pinch salt
2 packets stevia

Directions:

1) In a bowl, combine the almond milk, Greek yogurt, cocoa powder, salt, and stevia. Mix until well combined.
2) In another bowl, mix the remaining ingredients until well combined.
3) In 14 mini muffin liners, spray cooking spray and pour in the chocolate mixture. Top with peanut butter mixture. Repeat layers.
4) Place in the freezer and freeze for 2 hours.

Nutrition Information:
Calories per serving: 120; Protein: 2.5g; Carbs: 16.4g; Fat: 5.1g Sugar: 5.9g

Chipotle Mac and Cheese Waffles

Serves: 2
Cooking Time: 10 minutes

Ingredients:
2 sachets Optavia Select Chipotle Mac and Cheese
4 ounces cold water
6 tablespoons liquid egg whites
Cooking spray
1 teaspoon hot sauce
2 tablespoon sugar-free maple syrup

Directions:
1) In a medium-sized microwave-safe bowl, mix the Chipotle Mac and Cheese with water. Mix until well combined.
2) Microwave on high for 1 ½ minutes. Let it stand for 1 minute. Repeat three times. Allow to cool and whisk in the liquid egg whites.
3) Pour the mixture into greased waffle iron. Close the lid and bake for 5 minutes until cooked. Remove from the waffle iron and serve with hot sauce and maple syrup.

Nutrition Information:
Calories per serving: 242; Protein: 17.9g; Carbs: 5.7g; Fat: 17.3g Sugar: 2.7g

Tiramisu Milkshake

Serves: 1
Cooking Time: 5 minutes

Ingredients:
1 sachet Optavia Frosty Coffee Soft Serve Treat
½ cup ice
6 ounces plain low-fat Greek yogurt
½ cup almond milk
2 tablespoons sugar-free chocolate
2 tablespoons whipped topping

Directions:
1) Place all ingredients except the whipped topping in a blender.
2) Pulse until smooth.
3) Pour in glass and top with whipped topping.

Nutrition Information:
Calories per serving: 239; Protein: 23.7g; Carbs: 64.2g; Fat: 22.8g Sugar: 15.2g

Sweet Potato Pecan Muffins

Serves: 4
Cooking Time: 30 minutes

Ingredients:
2 sachets Optavia Select Honey Sweet Potatoes
1 cup cold water
2 sachets Optavia Essential Spiced Gingerbread
6 tablespoons liquid egg substitute
¼ cup unsweetened almond milk
½ teaspoon pumpkin pie spice
½ teaspoon vanilla extract
½ teaspoon baking powder
Cooking spray
1 1/3 ounces chopped pecans

Directions:
1) Preheat the oven to 350°F.
2) Prepare the Honey Sweet Potatoes according to package directions. Allow to cool.
3) In a bowl, combine the cooked Honey Sweet Potatoes and the remaining ingredients (except for the pecan).
4) Divide mixture in four muffin cups and sprinkle with pecans.
5) Bake for 20 minutes.

Nutrition Information:
Calories per serving: 211; Protein: 5.5g; Carbs: 32.7g; Fat: 7.2g Sugar: 11.6g

Shake Cake

Serves: 1
Cooking Time: 20 minutes

Ingredients:
1 shake packet
¼ teaspoon baking powder
2 tablespoons egg beaters
2 tablespoons water
1 tablespoon reduced fat cream cheese
½ packet Splenda

Directions:
1) Preheat the oven to 350°F.
2) Mix all ingredients in a bowl.
3) Pour in a muffin cup and bake for 15 minutes.
4) Allow to cool.

Nutrition Information:
Calories per serving: 271; Protein: 8.7g; Carbs: 19.4g; Fat: 7.9g Sugar: 12.7g

Pumpkin Chocolate Cheesecake

Serves: 1
Cooking Time: 60 minutes

Ingredients:
2 sachets Optavia Essential Decadent Double Chocolate Brownie
½ tablespoon unsalted butter, melted
2 tablespoons cold water
Cooking spray
1 cup non-fat plain Greek yogurt
3 tablespoons light cream cheese, softened
3 tablespoons pumpkin puree
2 packets stevia
½ teaspoon pumpkin pie spice
½ teaspoon salt
Vanilla extract

Directions:
1) Preheat the oven to 350°F.
2) In bowl, combine the Chocolate Brownies, butter, and water.
3) Divide the brownie mixture into two mini spring form pans. Press the mixture in the bottom of the pan to create a crust.
4) Bake for 15 minutes.
5) Meanwhile, combine the remaining ingredients in a bowl and mix until smooth. Divide mixture evenly among the two spring-form pans.
6) Lower the temperature to 300°F. Bake for 40 minutes.

Nutrition Information:
Calories per serving: 298; Protein: 10.1g; Carbs: 5.5g; Fat: 17.2g Sugar: 1.9g

Cinnamon Bun Blondies

Serves: 4
Cooking Time: 30 minutes

Ingredients:
4 sachets Optavia Cinnamon Cream Cheese Swirl Cake
½ teaspoon cinnamon
½ teaspoon baking powder
2/3 cup unsweetened almond milk
2 tablespoons unsalted butter, melted
3 tablespoons liquid egg whites, divided
1 1/3 ounces pecans, chopped
Cooking spray
¼ cup light cream cheese, softened
1 packet sugar substitute
½ teaspoon vanilla extract

Directions:
1) Preheat the oven to 350°F.
2) In a bowl, combine the Cinnamon Cream Cheese Swirl Cake, cinnamon, and baking powder. Add the milk, butter and half of the liquid egg whites. Stir to combine. Fold in the pecans.
3) Pour the batter into greased loaf pan.
4) In a bowl, combine the rest of the ingredients until well-combined. Dollop the cream cheese mixture and swirl using a knife.
5) Bake for 20 minutes until the batter is set.

Nutrition Information:
Calories per serving: 179; Protein: 4.6g; Carbs: 4.8g; Fat: 16.3g Sugar: 3.8g

Tropical Chia Seed Pudding

Serves: 2
Cooking Time: 5minutes

Ingredients:
2 sachets Optavia Chia Bliss Smoothie
¼ cup chia seeds
1 cup unsweetened coconut milk
½ teaspoon lemon zest

Directions:
1) Combine all ingredients in a bowl and stir until well-combined.
2) Pour mixture into glass jars and keep in the fridge overnight.

Nutrition Information:
Calories per serving: 323; Protein: 14.1g; Carbs: 23.8g; Fat: 20.1g Sugar: 6.2g

Chicago Style Snack Mix

Serves: 1
Cooking Time: 5 minutes

Ingredients:
½ sachet Optavia Sharp Cheddar & Sour Cream Popcorn
½ sachet Optavia Puffed Sweet and Salty Snacks
1 teaspoon Walden Farms Caramel Syrup
1 teaspoon grated parmesan cheese

Directions:
1) Combine the Sharp Cheddar & Sour Cream Popcorn and Puffed Sweet & Salty Snacks in a resealable bag. Drizzle with syrup and sprinkle with cheese.
2) Toss to coat.

Nutrition Information:
Calories per serving: 215; Protein:14.2 g; Carbs: 43.3g; Fat: 6.3g Sugar: 6.1g

Sweet Potato Muffins

Serves: 1
Cooking Time: minutes

Ingredients:
1 sachet Optavia Honey Sweet Potatoes
½ cup water
2 tablespoons egg beaters
¼ teaspoon baking powder
A pinch of cinnamon

Directions:
1) Preheat the oven to 350°F.
2) In a bowl, stir the sweet potato, water, egg beaters, and baking powder.
3) Pour into greased muffin cups and sprinkle with cinnamon.
4) Bake for 15 minutes.

Nutrition Information:
Calories per serving: 239; Protein: 12.2g; Carbs: 26.1g; Fat: 9.2g Sugar: 8.1g

Grasshopper Parfaits

Serves: 1
Cooking Time: 10 minutes

Ingredients:

1 sachet Optavia Essential Decadent Double Chocolate Brownie
1 sachet Optavia Essential Creamy Vanilla Shake
¼ cup plain low-fat Greek yogurt
¼ cup unsweetened cashew milk
¼ teaspoon peppermint extract
Green food coloring
¼ cup pressurized whipped topping

Directions:

1) Cook the Decadent Double Chocolate Brownie according to package instructions. Allow to cool and crumble into small pieces.
2) In a bowl, combine the creamy vanilla shake, yogurt, milk, peppermint, and a drop of green food coloring. Mix until smooth.
3) Assemble by layering the brownie mixture and milk mixture on top of one another.
4) Top with whipped cream.

Nutrition Information:

Calories per serving: 471; Protein: 11.5g; Carbs: 28.2g; Fat: 37.4g Sugar: 19.2g

CPSIA information can be obtained
at www.ICGtesting.com
Printed in the USA
LVHW060238261020
669807LV00008B/133

Ce livre appartient à

____

Conception des jeux : Agnès Lechat

ISBN : 978-2-7470-4598-8

18 rue Barbès – 92120 Montrouge – France
Dépôt légal : février 2013 – Deuxième édition
Imprimé en Chine
Loi 49-956 du 16 juillet 1949 sur les publications destinées à la jeunesse

Serge Bloch • Nicolas Hubesch

ZOUK

sorcières de mère en fille

bayard jeunesse

Dans une grande, très grande ville du bout du monde,
au milieu des grands, très grands immeubles,
il y a une petite, toute petite maison.

C’est là qu’habitent Zouk et sa famille.

Zouk est une charmante
petite fille, comme toutes
les petites filles.

Son papa, Saluléga,
a une grosse voiture,
comme tous les papas.

Sa jolie maman, Salsepareille,
est la plus gentille, la plus douce
et la plus drôle des mamans.

Et voici ses deux amis,
Noyau et monsieur Potiron.

C’est une famille comme les autres. Enfin… presque !
Car, dans cette famille-là, on est tous sorciers !
Mais ne le dites à personne, c’est un secret.

ABRACADABRI, CADABRA

ZOUK

sorcières de mère en fille

Leçon de potion

Dans la grande, très grande ville, Zouk a décidé d'apprendre à fabriquer des potions magiques avec sa maman, Salsepareille.

– On va commencer par la potion qui rend fort, dit Salsepareille.
Dans cette marmite, il faut mettre trois poils de carotte, deux larmes de crocodile,
un peu de bave d'escargot et une vieille chaussure.

On fait cuire à feu doux en remuant, et on récite la formule magique.

– Est-ce que je peux goûter ? demande Zouk.
– Oui, mais juste une petite cuillerée, sinon, c'est dangereux ! répond Salsepareille.

– Pouah ! C'est vraiment mauvais ! dit Zouk. Elle commence à sentir un petit picotement dans son ventre... Le picotement devient un chatouillis, et Zouk se sent très forte, si forte qu'elle peut porter la marmite qui lui semble aussi légère qu'une frite !

Mais Zouk est une petite sorcière qui a du caractère. Elle en veut encore et, dès que sa maman a le dos tourné, elle avale toute la louche... Et BOUM! Elle bondit dans tous les sens et traverse le plafond.

Elle soulève un camion, elle saute plus haut que le plus haut des gratte-ciel,

elle soulève la plus grande des grandes statues de la grande, très grande ville.
Tout le monde a très peur, mais...

Salsepareille, qui est la sorcière la plus forte de la Terre,
arrive et dit une formule magique :

Zouk se fait un peu gronder, puis pardonner.
Et elle promet de ne plus recommencer…
jusqu'à la prochaine fois !

Les courses avec maman

Dans la grande, très grande ville, Zouk la petite sorcière qui a du caractère
et sa maman chérie adorée partent faire des courses.
Salsepareille dit à Zouk : – On va t'habiller de la tête aux pieds.
Mais Zouk n'a pas envie, elle se trouve très bien comme elle est.

Salsepareille et Zouk prennent l'ascenseur. Au 12e étage, tout le monde descend. Sauf Zouk, Salsepareille et quelques sorciers qui montent au 13e étage, l'étage secret réservé aux sorciers.

C'est l'étage préféré de Zouk. Salsepareille dit : – Tu as grandi, il faut t'acheter un nouveau balai. Zouk essaie un balai jaune vraiment trop grand, et un balai gris vraiment trop petit. Finalement, Zouk va garder son balai chéri.

Au rayon « chapeaux », Zouk en essaie plein. Mais elle n'en trouve pas un qui lui plaise. – Ils sont tous nuls, je veux un chapeau pointu! La vendeuse dit : – Désolée, mademoiselle, nous n'avons plus que des chapeaux carrés. – J'ai horreur des carrés, grogne Zouk.

Zouk et Salsepareille vont alors au rayon « beauté ». Zouk essaie tous les parfums : Chou pourri, Bave d'escargot, Queue de radis, Crotte d'asticot et Pipi de crapaud. Elle s'asperge. Quelle horreur, toutes ces odeurs qui se mélangent!

Zouk essaie des Radimoches qui clignotent,
des Kaïkaï en imitation peau de serpent.

Puis Zouk veut voir plein d'autres chaussures. La vendeuse est épuisée et Salsepareille en a vraiment assez. – Décide-toi, Zouk !
Zouk dit : – Je veux des Blingbling à ressorts, les mêmes que ma cousine !
Évidemment, il n'y en a plus.

Dans les autres rayons, Zouk essaie encore des tas d'habits. Mais les pantalons sont trop longs, les robes sont toutes moches et les baguettes ne sont pas chouettes. – Il est nul, ton magasin, Maman, dit Zouk, il n'y a rien!

Salsepareille n'en peut plus : – Rentrons, Zouk, c'est un cauchemar de faire des courses avec toi! Zouk, ravie, dit : – Maman, c'est promis, je ne recommencerai plus... jusqu'à la prochaine fois!

Leçon de transformation

C'est les vacances. Salsepareille, la sorcière la plus forte de la Terre va apprendre à Zouk, sa fille chérie, quelques tours de sorcellerie.

– Apprends-moi à me transformer en ce que je veux! dit Zouk.
– Encore! dit Salsepareille. Mais tu es très bien comme tu es!
– Non, non, insiste Zouk. Je veux me transformer!

– Bon, d'accord, dit Salsepareille, alors commençons par la potion : trois grains de perlimpinpin, trois patates pourries et trois gouttes de pipi de mammouth. Trois minutes au micro-ondes et voilà.
Alors... vous voulez être transformés en quoi?

– Moi, dit monsieur Potiron, je voudrais être mince et beau comme… comme un poireau !

– Moi, dit Noyau, je voudrais être grand et costaud comme un lion, le roi des animaux.

– Et moi, dit Zouk, je veux être une princesse pour avoir un prince charmant à moi toute seule.

Chacun boit trois gouttes de potion pendant que Salsepareille prononce la formule magique.

Chacun est transformé en ce qu'il voulait.

Mais bientôt, Noyau est très malheureux : chaque fois qu'il ouvre la bouche, il casse les oreilles à tout le monde.

Monsieur Potiron, lui aussi, est malheureux. Il dit :
– J'ai l'air idiot, moi, en poireau !

Et Zouk est la plus malheureuse de tous. Elle n'aime ni sa robe, ni sa couronne de diamants...
– J'ai même pas de prince charmant.

Zouk supplie : – On veut redevenir comme avant, s'il te plaît, Maman...
– Tu vois, je te l'avais dit, bougonne Salsepareille.
Attention, je vais prononcer la formule magique !

Et voilà, quel bonheur ! Zouk est si heureuse d'être redevenue Zouk !
Monsieur Potiron est si heureux d'être redevenu tout rond,
et Noyau est si heureux de pouvoir miauler comme avant !

Alors Zouk promet de ne plus se transformer… jusqu'à la prochaine fois !

Gare à mamie Zak!

Dreling! Dreling! On sonne à la porte. Zouk regarde par la fenêtre : c'est mamie Zak qui vient la garder pendant que ses parents sont à un congrès de sorciers.

– Coucou ma chérie! Je suis ravie de garder ma petite-fille préférée.

Zouk aime bien sa grand-mère, même si ce n'est pas facile depuis qu'elle a adopté Raymond, un cochon aussi sale que mal élevé.

Et mamie Zak n'aime que lui!

Ça, ça va encore, mais ce que Zouk ne supporte pas, c'est que mamie Zak donne des ordres tout le temps.

En plus, Zouk doit s'occuper de ce cochon mal léché. Pendant que mamie est allée se reposer, elle doit lui brosser le dos, lui donner un gâteau et supporter ses gros mots.

Alors ça, c'est vraiment trop. Zouk dit une formule magique :

Et l'horrible Raymond est aussitôt transformé en un rat rose et gras…

… que Noyau s'empresse d'avaler comme un vulgaire hamburger. Bon débarras !

Mais quand mamie Zak découvre que son petit chéri a disparu… rien ne va plus.

Quelle émotion! Une vraie inondation! Soudain, on entend une petite voix qui sort du ventre du chat : – Mamie… je suis là…
Mamie Zak attrape Noyau et dit :

Vite, Zouk prononce une formule magique :

Raymond redevient un cochon. Mamie Zak est contente de le retrouver. Zouk se fait gronder, puis pardonner.

Et Zouk promet de ne plus recommencer... jusqu'à la prochaine fois !

On a perdu mamie Zak

Mamie Zak, la grand-mère de Zouk, vient d'arriver. Et comme d'habitude, elle est accompagnée de son inséparable cochon préféré, l'horrible Raymond. Zouk est désespérée.

Soudain, mamie Zak crie : – Assez paressé ! Raymond et moi, nous avons besoin d'un peu d'exercice. Et toi aussi, ma petite. Allons nous promener !

Et les voilà gambadant gaiement dans le grand, très grand parc, de la grande, très grande ville.

Zouk trouve que promener un cochon en laisse, ce n'est pas facile du tout.

Parfois, il ne veut pas avancer.

Parfois, il faut l'arrêter.

Parfois, il a de drôles d'idées.

Et parfois, il faut même le porter.

Mais le plus désagréable, c'est qu'il faut que Zouk ramasse ses crottes,
et Raymond est vraiment un cochon.

Quelle corvée!

Alors là, c'est la crotte qui fait déborder le vase. Zouk crie : – ASSEEEEEEEEEZ! J'en ai assez de ton cochon, mamie Zak! Je m'en vais!

Mais sans Zouk, mamie Zak et Raymond se perdent dans le grand parc.
La nuit tombe. Que vont-ils devenir?

Ils entendent des cris effrayants. Est-ce que ce sont des loups?
Vont-ils dévorer ce pauvre Raymond et peut-être mamie Zak aussi?
Car les loups sont gourmands. Les cris se rapprochent…

Ce ne sont pas des loups, mais les sirènes des voitures de police.
Zouk, sur son balai, leur montre le chemin.

Ouf! Mamie est sauvée. C'est Zouk qui a appelé la police.
Elle se fait un peu gronder, puis pardonner.

Et elle promet de ne plus recommencer... jusqu'à la prochaine fois!

Bonne nuit les petits

Comme tous les soirs, Zouk met son pyjama préféré.
Celui avec des araignées.

Zouk se brosse les dents avec son dentifrice à la bave de crapaud.

Zouk fait un petit pipi de sorcière...
Et ZOU, au lit !

Puis Salsepareille, la plus gentille des mamans sorcières,
lui raconte une histoire de monstres horribles et d'ogres féroces.

Zouk préférerait une histoire de prince charmant,
parce qu'elle rêve d'être une princesse.

Salsepareille lui fait un petit bisou, et son papa Saluléga lui en fait un gros.

Et CLIC, on éteint la lumière. Dors bien, petite Zouk...

Mais Zouk est une petite sorcière qui a du caractère.
Elle prononce une formule magique.

Aussitôt, toutes sortes de monstres rigolos apparaissent.
Il y a Chico, Cornio, Costo, Croco, Zozo…

C'est la fête ! Zouk fait la folle avec tous ses amis. Ils font un bruit d'enfer.

Salsepareille et Saluléga se demandent ce qui se passe.
Malheur, on attaque leur fille chérie.
– N'aie pas peur, nous arrivons ! crie Saluléga.

Mais quand ils ouvrent la porte, tout est normal. Enfin presque...

Des parents sorciers, c'est plus malin que ça !
Et Zouk promet de ne plus recommencer... jusqu'à la prochaine fois !

Joue avec Zouk

La formule magique

Pour faire une potion qui rend tous les monstres mignons,
Zouk a besoin de retrouver les ingrédients qui se terminent par le son « ON ».
Tu peux l'aider ?

Bravo ! Maintenant, entraîne-toi à dire trois de ces mots à la queue leu leu
et, si tu rencontres un monstre, ajoute à la fin :
« Par le pouvoir de mes abracadamots, deviens abracamignon ! »

Les drôles d'animots

Moi, je fais de la magie avec les mots.
Et voilà ! Cela fait de drôles d'animaux.
Retrouve-les dans l'image. Il y a le radinosaure, la girafleur, le lézarc-en-ciel, le crapotiron, le pissenlion, le coquelicochon, la tortulipe, la vachemise, le lézartichaut, le serpendule et l'éléphantôme.

Le magazine **Les Belles HISTOIRES** *publie chaque mois une nouvelle aventure de Zouk!*